R · W · LIGHTBOWN

DONATELLO AND MICHELOZZO

IN TWO VOLUMES
VOLUME II : ILLUSTRATIONS
NOTES · DOCUMENTS

DONATELLO AND MICHELOZZO
is published in two volumes
Volume I contains the Text
Volume II contains Illustrations, Notes, Documents,
Glossary, Tables and Index

R·W·LIGHTBOWN

DONATELLO & MICHELOZZO

An Artistic Partnership and its Patrons

in the Early Renaissance

Volume II ꞉ Illustrations
Notes and Documents

HARVEY MILLER LONDON

Published by Harvey Miller
20 Marryat Road · London SW19 5BD · England

Distribution: Heyden & Son Ltd., Spectrum House,
Hillview Gardens, London NW4 2JQ, England;
247 South 41st St., Philadelphia PA 19104, USA;
Münsterstrasse 22, 4440 Rheine/Westf., Germany.

ISBN 0 905203 22 4 (SET OF TWO VOLUMES)
ISBN 0 905203 27 5 (VOLUME ONE)
ISBN 0 905203 28 3 (VOLUME TWO)

Printed in Great Britain
Text printed by Latimer Trend & Company Ltd
Crescent Avenue · Plymouth · England
Illustrations originated by Roger Adams · London EC4
Printed by Cheney & Sons Ltd · Banbury

CONTENTS

VOLUME TWO

CONTENTS OF VOLUME ONE

NOTES TO THE TEXT

Abbreviations

Burger   F. Burger. *Geschichte des florentinischen Grabmals von den
                        ältesten Zeiten bis Michelangelo.* Strasburg, 1904.

Fabriczy   C. von Fabriczy, 'Michelozzo di Bartolommeo', in *Jahr-
                        buch der Königlich Preussischen Kuntsammlungen*, XXV,
                        1904, Beiheft, pp. 34–110.

Janson   H. W. Janson. *The sculpture of Donatello.* 2 vols. Prince-
                        ton, 1957.

Longhurst   M. H. Longhurst. *Notes on Italian monuments of the 12th
                        to 16th centuries.* 2 vols., privately printed, London, 1961.

Morisani   O. Morisani. *Michelozzo architetto.* Turin, 1951.

Venturi, *Storia*   A. Venturi, *Storia dell'arte italiana*, 1901–40.

Wolff   F. Wolff. *Michelozzo di Bartolommeo. Ein Beitrag zur
                        Geschichte der Architektur und Plastik im Quattrocento.*
                        Strasburg, 1900.

Notes to the Text

NOTES TO PROLOGUE

1. The documents concerning Michelozzo's life or work were collected by Fabriczy (see abbreviations) in 1904. Unless a different source is given, it is from his article that they have been cited. The *portate al catasto* or tax returns which are one of the principal sources for our knowledge of Michelozzo's work were retranscribed, not altogether accurately, by R. Graves Mather ('New documents on Michelozzo,' in *Art Bulletin*, XXIV, 1942, pp. 226–31) who seems to have been unaware of Fabriczy's previous publication. They have since been transcribed by H. M. Caplow, *Michelozzo*, ii, London & New York, 1977, pp. 644–60 who has added transcripts of new documents.

The dating of the *portate al catasto* has as usual been confused by failure to make use of historical evidence or to take account of the Florentine style of dating. This has led in particular to a confused use of Michelozzo's *portate* of 1427 and of 1430 (really 1431). For the latter see the discussion in Chapter VII. With regard to the former, from which we first learn that Michelozzo and Donatello had been partners for *due anni o incircha* (Fabriczy, p. 62), we know that it was drawn up at the same time as or before Donatello's *portata* of 11 July 1427, which Michelozzo made out for him (see n. 5). It cannot have been made out before 22 May 1427, the date when the *provvigione* imposing the *catasto* was passed, and must in fact be rather later than this first possible date, probably later in fact than 28 June, when new regulations were made for the *catasto* (see O. Karmin, *La legge del castato fiorentino del 1427*, Florence, 1906). It should be noted that only on 4 July did the Ufficiali del Catasto decide that the citizens could be *accastati* in whatever *gonfalone* they chose.

For the problem of the partnership of Donatello and Michelozzo see especially H. von Geymüller, 'Die architektonische Entwicklung Michelozzos und sein Zusammenwirken mit Donatello' in *Jahrbuch der K. Preussischen Kunstsammlungen*, xi, 1894, pp. 247–59; Bode, 'Donatello als Architekt und Dekorator,' *ib.*, xxii, 1901, pp. 3–28; *id.*, *Florentiner Bildhauer der Renaissance*, Berlin, 1902, pp. 17–70; Wolff; H. Stegmann, 'Michelozzo di Bartolommeo' in Stegmann and Geymüller, *Die Architektur der Renaissance in Toscana*, Munich, 1885–1907; Morisani; V. Martinelli, 'Donatello e Michelozzo a Roma' in *Commentari*, viii, 1957, pp. 167–94, ix, 1958, pp. 3–24: *id.*, 'La "compagnia" di Donatello e di Michelozzo e la sepoltura del Brancacci a Napoli,' in *Commentari*, xiv, 1963, pp. 211–26; H. M. Caplow, 'Sculptors' partnerships in Michelozzo's Florence,' in *Studies in the Renaissance*, xxi, 1974, pp. 145–73.

2. R. Graves Mather, 'Donatello debitore oltre la tomba', in *Rivista d'Arte*, xix, 1937, pp. 186–7; I. Orsini, *Storia delle monete della repubblica fiorentina*, Florence, 1760, pp. 156–208.

3. See R. Krautheimer and T. Krautheimer-Hess, *Lorenzo Ghiberti*, Princeton, 1970, i, pp. 86–7, ii, pp. 406–99. G. B. Gelli, (ed. G. Mancini, 'Vite d'artisti di Giovanni Battista Gelli', in *Archivio storico italiano*, ser. 5, xvii, 1896, p. 61) attributed the St. Matthew wholly to Michelozzo.

4. Fabriczy, p. 61.

5. Donatello's *portata al castato* of 11 July 1427, was made out for him by Michelozzo (printed in R. Graves Mather, 'Donatello debitore oltre la tomba', in *Rivista d'Arte*, xix, 1937, pp. 181–92). For Michelozzo's see Fabriczy, pp. 61–3.

NOTES TO CHAPTER I

1. F. Gregorovius, *The tombs of the Popes*, trans. R. Seton-Watson, London, 1903, p. 70.

2. The literature on Cossa is poor and vitiated

by partisan prejudice or by want of historical perspective. General works are C. Hunger, *Zur Geschichte Papst Johanns XXIII*, Bonn, 1876; E. J. Kitts, *In the days of the Councils: a sketch of the life and times of Baldassare Cossa*, London, 1908; *id.*, *Pope John the Twenty-Third and Master John Hus of Bohemia*, London, 1910. Specialist studies which print or refer to documents that have an important bearing on Cossa's career are A. Esch, *Bonifaz IX und der Kirchenstaat*, Tübingen, 1969; *id.*, 'Das Papsttum unter der Herrschaft der Neapolitaner', in *Festschrift für Hermann Heimpel*, ii, Göttingen, 1972, pp. 713–800; G. Gozzadini, *Nanne Gozzadini e Baldassare Cossa poi Giovanni XXIII*, Bologna, 1880; G. Holmes, 'How the Medici became the Pope's bankers', in *Florentine Studies*, ed. N. Rubinstein, London, 1968, pp. 57–80; H. G. Peter, *Die Informationen Papst Johanns XXIII and dessen Flucht von Konstanz bis Schaffhausen*, Freiburg im B., 1926; H. Finke, 'Flucht und Schicksale Johannes XXIII in badischen Landen', in *Bilder vom Konstanzer Konzil*, Heidelberg, 1903, pp. 7–59.

3. For Cossa's return to Italy and submission to Martin see G. Canestrini, in 'Vita di Bartolommeo Valori (il Vecchio),' in *Archivio storico italiano*, iv, 1843, pp. 429–38; Finke, *Acta Concilii Constanciensis*, iii, pp. 291 ff; Rymer, *Foedera*, iv, pt. 2, 1740, pp. 121–2; *Commissioni di Rinaldo degli Albizzi*, ed. C. Guasti, i, pp. 298, 303–4, 307; H. Korner, *Die Chronica Novella*, ed. J. Schwalm, 1895, pp. 422–3; anonymous life of Martin in *Liber Pontificalis*, ed. Duchesne, pp. 518–19; *Carteggio di Guido Manfredi Cancelliere della Repubblica di Lucca*, in R. Archivio di Stato, Lucca, *Regesti*, iii, pt. 2, 1933, pp. 83–4, 88, 89, 91, 93, 96–7; Holmes, *op. cit.*, pp. 375–6; the Diary of Cardinal Fillastre, in Finke, *op. cit.*, i, pp. 169–70; Filippo Rinuccini, *Ricordi storici*, ed. G. Aiazzi, Florence, 1840, p. lviii; Domenico di Lionardo Boninsegni, *Storia della Città di Firenze Dall'Anno 1410 al 1460*, Florence, 1637, p. 15; Sercambi, *Le croniche*, ed. Bongi, iii, 1892, pp. 241–2; Finke, *op. cit.*, iii, pp. 295–6, 299–305.

4. For his residence in Florence and death see B. del Corazza, *Diario*, printed by G. O. Corazzini, 'Diario fiorentino di Bartolommeo di Michele del Corazza', in *Archivio storico italiano*, ser. 5, xiv, 1894, pp. 263–4; Fillastre, *loc. cit.*, giving date of death as Saturday 23 December

and the time as 'in the morning.' Del Corazza, *loc. cit.*, gives the same day but in November, time as *ore 12*. 22 December is the date of the epitaph, and is also the date given by Rinuccini, Boninsegni and Ammirato. The house in which he died was later known as Palazzo Orlandini.

5. For Martin's licence to Cossa to make a will (a licence demanded by canon law) see Esch, 1972, p. 779, n. 241. A first draft of the will, dated 21 December, is printed by Richa, *Notizie istoriche delle chiese fiorentine*, v, 1757, pp. xxxvii–viii. The final will is printed by G. Canestrini, 'Vita di Bartolommeo Valori (il Vecchio)', in *Archivio storico italiano*, iv, 1843, pp. 292–96, together with a number of documents connected with Cossa's release.

6. Del Migliore, *Firenze città nobilissima*, Florence, 1684, p. 95; G. Sercambi, *Le croniche*, ed. S. Bongi, iii, 1892, pp. 248–9. Sercambi records the usual rumours of poisoning as the cause of his death.

7. Del Migliore, *op. cit*, p. 103; Richa, *vol. cit.*, pp. xlviii–l, citing 'an ancient parchment' then in the custody of the *Arte di Calimala*.

8. Farullo, *Istoria cronologica del Monastero degli Angioli di Firenze*, 1710, p. 39, for Cosimo's intervention with John to procure a bull exempting S. M. degli Angioli from all Papal levies; Richa, *op. cit.*, viii, 1759, pp. 159–60; Holmes, *op. cit.*, p. 373.

9. See the documents of March 1419 by which Martin orders the surrender of registers and mitre in Finke, iii, pp. 291–2. Scipione Ammirato, *Delle famiglie nobili napoletane Parte Seconda*, Florence, 1651, p. 287. Marino left her dowry, as was usual, to his wife Caterina, a *barletta* of silver to Pietro, Michele's little son, 'la quale era in mano di Bartolommeo da Montegonsi cittadino fiorentino', a silver flask to Giovanni. He also made pious bequests '& in particolare alla cappella posta in Santa Maria d'Ischia, dove dice esser sepolto D. Giouanni Coscia suo padre.' The will, *rogato da Ser Giuliano di Colino da San Giusto*, is dated 21 October 1418 Pisan style, i.e. 1417 Florentine and modern style.

10. *Cronica di Buonaccorso Pitti*, ed. A. Bacchi della Lega, Bologna, 1905, pp. 155–62. Altopascio was the head convent of an order of Augustinian friars whose chief obligation was to lodge and serve pilgrims.

11. For Bartolommeo Valori see Canestrini (*op. cit.*). The anecdotes about John occur on pp. 247, 248–9 (where Eugenius IV is mistakenly named in place of John), 262 (episode wrongly placed in Florence). For his mission to Ferrara with Giovanni de' Medici in February 1414, when both were members of the Dieci, see H. Herre, in *Quellen und Forschungen*, iv, 1902, p. 61.

12. For Vieri Guadagni see L. Passerini, *Genealogia e storia della Famiglia Guadagni*, Florence, 1873, pp. 54–65.

13. See his letter printed in Appendix A, doc. 3.

14. Del Corazza, *op. cit.*, pp. 264–7, from whom the rest of the account of the funeral exequies is taken, except where otherwise indicated.

15. According to M. M. Newett, *Canon Pietro Casola's Pilgrimage to Jerusalem in the year 1494*, Manchester, 1907, p. 148, a *doppiero* was a torch formed of several wax candles fastened together. I have rendered it as 'torch'.

16. See Appendix A, doc. 2.

17. The name of the Cardinal is left blank by Del Corazza, but it was certainly Cossa's nephew Tommaso Brancaccio.

18. Amerigo Corsini. Del Corazza calls him an Archbishop; hence his account must have been compiled – at any rate in its final form – after 2 May 1420, when Martin raised Florence to the rank of archbishopric. Giovanni de' Medici, letter of 31 December 1419, *cit.* in n. 13. For the custom of offering palls for the souls of the deceased see F. Michel, *Recherches sur le commerce, la fabrication et l'usage des étoffes de soie. . . .*, i, 1852, pp. 145–48.

19. Ammirato, *Istorie fiorentine*, Pt. I, ii, Florence, 1647, p. 985.

20. For Michele's letter see Appendix A, doc. 4. Giovanni's is in Archivio di Stato, Florence, Mediceo avanti il Principato, Filza I, no. 236. The existence of these letters was first made known by Holmes, *op. cit.*, p. 376.

21. Ammirato, *loc. cit.*

22. See Appendix A, doc. 5. As a result of a mistaken interpretation of a note by Senatore Carlo Strozzi (Archivio di Stato, Florence, Manoscritti Strozziani, ser. 3, Cod. 250, *Bozze di uarie cose*, f. 115v–116) who invariably keeps to the old Florentine style in his notes, the year is always mistakenly given as 1420. For the bibliography of the reliquary see L. Becherucci, in L. Becherucci and G. Brunetti, *Il Museo dell' Opera del Duomo a Firenze*, ii, Florence, pp. 256–7, no. 26. For another relic of the Baptist's hand with a Byzantine provenance left to his family chapel in the Duomo by Cardinal Corsini in 1403 see *op. cit.*, pp. 239–40.

23. Del Migliore, *op. cit.*, p. 103.

24. F. Albertini, *Memoriale di molte statve et picture*, ed. Horne, London, 1909, p. 8.

25. Archivio di Stato, Florence, Carte Strozziane, ser. 2, Cod. 51.3, *Spoglio terzo delle Scritture dell' Arte di Calimala*, f. 6 (2) '*A Gio: del Chiaro Orafo si paga f. 40 per l'Opera di S. Gio. per dorare l'orliquia del Dito di S. Gio. per la metà che tocca a lei. Libro Grande d'Arte S^{to} F 1421 231*'; f. 6v. '*Mr. Baldassar Coscia lasciò f. 200 per adornare il Reliquiere del dito di S. Gio. b.^{a} Si spende f. 280 e si pagano a Gio. del Chiaro Orefice 1423 filza dal 1414 al 1433.*' *Spoglio terzo*, f. 117. '*A Giovanni del Chiaro orefice si paga f. 200 per la Reliquiera del Dito di S. Gio. bat^a 1423 filza dal 1414 al 1433.*'

26. The document cited in what follows has been known since C. J. Cavallucci published it in 1888 in *Arte e storia*, vii, 1888, p. 36, from a summary of it in the Carte Strozziane which was made in the seventeenth century by the Senatore Carlo Strozzi. It should be emphasised that it is not the original, but Strozzi's version of the original. It was republished by Frey (in his edition of Vasari, I, i, Munich, 1911, p. 341, with wrong date of 1420) and again by M. Lisner, 'Zur frühen Bildhauer-Architektur Donatellos', in *Münchner Jahrbuch der bildenden Kunst*, ser. 3, ix–x, 1958–9, p. 117. But except for Dr. Lisner every scholar who has used it has without exception assumed that its date is new style, whereas Strozzi invariably keeps to the Florentine style of the document he is summarising or transcribing (for

259

obvious reasons, since he was making notes from the originals and needed the original dates for easy verification of his references). In his usage 9 January 1421 is equivalent to 9 January 1422. The document is transcribed again with the date 1421 in *Carte Strozziane*, ser. 2, Cod. 51.3, f. 11 (old numeration 3) as from '*filza 2da dal 1425 al 1438*'.

27. St. Thomas Aquinas, *Summa theologica*, 2–2, xxxii, art. 2; 3-supplementum, lxxi, arts. 2, 11.

28. A. M. Romanini, *Arnolfo di Cambio*, Milan, 1969, p. 53, n. 46.

29. Duchesne, ii, p. 235. Hugues's tomb was in fact executed ('*une table de cuivre . . . à main gauche est proche du grand Autel de Sainte Sabine,*' *op. cit.*, p. 246); *ib.*, pp. 279–80.

30. G. Mollat, 'Contribution à l'histoire du Sacré Collège' in *Revue d'histoire ecclésiastique*, xlvi, 1941, p. 591.

31. See Appendix A, doc. 7; for interment as a good work see Aquinas, *loc. cit.*

32. Vasari, *Vite*, ed. Milanesi, ii, 1878, p. 399; for Giovanni's retirement see De Roover, *op. cit.*

33. See Appendix A, doc. 6. Discovered and published by Dr. M. Lisner, *op. cit.*, p. 117, no. 2, who, however, misread the year as 1425 (modern style).

34. Fabriczy, p. 62.

35. Del Migliore, *op. cit.*, p. 96. For the formula '*olim Papa*' as expressing the Florentine view that John had been lawful Pope compare the bull of Pope Martin himself, printed in Appendix A, doc. 1 with docs. 2 & 5 in the same Appendix.

36. It was compiled by D. Marzi, *La Cancelleria della Repubblica Fiorentina*, 1910, pp. 497–8.

37. For his term as notary in 1420 see also Richa (*op. cit.*, ii, p. 226). For all his terms see *Ricordi di Giovanni Morelli*, in *Delizie degli eruditi toscani*, xix, Florence, 1785, ed. P. Ildefonso di San Luigi, pp. 49–60, giving Piero di Lodovico Doffi as notary in January and

February 1420; p. 67, giving him as notary in November and December 1424. He was not notary again until March and April 1433, two years after Martin's death (*op. cit.*, p. 112).

38. Ammirato, *loc. cit.*

39. Archivio di Stato, Florence, *Carte Strozziane*, ser. 2, Cod. 51.2, f. 123v (119).

40. See n. 33.

41. Original of document about marble in Fabriczy, p. 46, trans. in Janson, p. 59; Fabriczy, p. 62.

42. Canestrini, *op. cit.*, pp. 278–81.

43. Strozzi, *Spoglio secondo*, cit., f. 76 (71v) '*Testamenti*'.

44. Strozzi, ms. cit., f. 83: '*Gioello che rimase nell' heredità di Mr. Baldassare Coscia già Papa Gio: XXIII e doppo Card.^{le} di S^{to} Eustachio il qual Gioello era appresso lo Spedalingo di Sta. Maria Nuoua si delibera che facerà opera che si uenda per i Consoli, e si facerà composizione per d^o. Gioello con Cosimo de Medici e con gli altri, e del prezzo di esso quella parte che è per toccare alla d^a. heredità se ne compri Crediti di Monte per l'Opera di S. Gio. alla quale s'aspetta 1433. Deliberazioni 1432 c. 143.*' f. 109 (104): '*Rendita di fiorini 1000 di Monte Commune per fare Paramenti de damasi ritratti dal Gioello di Mr. Baldassare Coscia. Libro Grande d'Arte. S^{to} L 1433 274.*' '*Gioello che che fu di Papa Gio, qual' era un rubino, Legato in mezzo a due Diamanti si uende a Cosimo de Medici che diceua appartenersi a lui i 7/24 per fiorini 300 in tutto ancorche altre uolte se ne fusse trouato molto più e del ritratto se ne douette fare adornamenti per l'Altare di S. Gio. 1432 Quaderno d^o (i.e. Quaderno di Ricordi dal 1429 al 1434) 136.*'

NOTES TO CHAPTER II

1. Giovanni Villani, *Cronica*, ii, Florence, 1823, p. 89.

2. Bernardino Corio, *L'historia di Milano*, ed. of 1646, Padua, p. 562.

3. Its only possible rivals are the two late fourteenth-century Bardi tombs in Santa Croce.

4. J. Coolidge ('Further observations on Masaccio's *Trinity*', in *Art Bulletin*, xlviii, 1966, p. 383) observes that the stone of the upper part is different, and suggests that all the part of the monument above the second pylon including the Virgin and Child and the canopy is a later addition made by Michelozzo to the original design. The marble for the tomb is known however to have been bought piecemeal, and although Michelozzo almost certainly saw the tomb through its last stage, which is correctly identified by Coolidge, he is most unlikely to have modified its original design.

5. For the Strozzi tomb see Lisner, 'Zur frühen Bildhauer-Architektur Donatellos', in *Münchner Jahrbuch der bildenden Kunst*, ser. 3, ix–x, 1958–9, pp. 94–101, 125. Dr. Lisner sees the hand of Donatello and his workshop in part of this tomb.

6. I give the heraldic colours of the Cossa arms after Mazzella, *Descrittione del Regno di Napoli*, Naples, 1601, p. 709. Del Corazza, a contemporary (*Diario cit.*, p. 275) says: '*L'arme sua era liste bianche e verde dal mezzo in giù, e una coscia da lato di sopra, gialla nel campo azzurro.*'

7. For *breve* see the article by V. Lazzarini quoted in n. 33, p. 149.

8. Archivio di Stato, Florence, Mediceo avanti il Principato, 165, f. 41r. A. Lisini, 'Papa Gregorio XII e i senesi,' in *Rassegna Nazionale*, xci, 1896, p. 282. The exact sum was 124 gold florins, l.2, sol. 18, d. 10.

9. Mrs. Diane Finiello Zervas is preparing a study of proportional systems used during the early *quattrocento* in which she will set out her discoveries about the module which governs the tomb and its application. Ghiberti's MS (in the Biblioteca Nazionale, Florence, Magl. Cl. XVII, 2) first published by Semper, *Donatello*, 1887, p. 44. See also R. Corwegh, 'Der Verfasser des kleinen Codex Ghiberti,' in *Mitteilungen des Kunsthistorischen Instituts in Florenz*, i, 1910, p. 171: O. Morisani, *Michelozzo architetto*, Turin, 1951, p. 24, fig. 4: Janson, p. 61.

10. But as H. Glasser points out ('The litigation concerning Luca della Robbia's Federighi

tomb', in *Mitteilungen des Kunsthistorischen Instituts in Florenz*, xiv, 1969–70, pp. 24–32) the last remains of the gilding of the Federighi tomb have disappeared within living memory.

11. Antonio Manetti, *Vita di Filippo di Ser Brunellesco*, Florence, 1927, p. 66. For the authorship of this book see J. Schlosser Magnino, *La letteratura artistica*, ed. O. Kurz, Florence and Vienna, 1964, pp. 115–16, with references.

12. Manetti, *op. cit.*, pp. 20–3; *loc. cit.*

13. Albertini, *Memoriale di molte statue et pictvre*, ed. Horne, London, 1909, p. 8.

14. Antonio Billi says '*Fece il sepolcro di papa Janni in Firenze, posto nella chiesa di San Giovannj, con tuttj 'e suoi hornamentj, excetto che una figura, di mano di Michelozzo, eccetto che* (sic e cioè) *una Fede, che ha uno callice in mano, et ha l'uno braccio minore che l'altro*' (Antonio Billi, *Il Libro*, ed. C. Frey, Berlin, 1892, pp. 42, 43: cf. the Anonimo Fiorentino, *Il Codice Magliabechiano*, ed. C. Frey, p. 77): Vasari, *Vite*, i, Florence, 1550, pp. 337–8.

15. G. Mancini, 'Vite d'artisti di Giovanni Battista Gelli,' in *Archivio storico italiano*, ser. v., xvii, 1896, p. 60 (source in part Billi).

16. For the iconography of Charity see R. Freyhan 'The evolution of the Caritas figure in the thirteenth and fourteenth centuries', in *Journal of the Warburg and Courtauld Institutes*, xi, 1948, pp. 68–86. D. D. Pincus ('A hand by Antonio Rizzo and the Double Caritas scheme of the Tron tomb,' in *Art Bulletin*, li, 1969, pp. 247–56) has some useful observations on the later development of Charity, but the evolution marked by Donatello's figure has escaped her notice.

17. The inscription on the Pazzi tomb reads: 'S(*epulchrum*) d(*omi*)ni Francisci et d(*omi*)ni Simonis de Pazzis et solummodo filiorum descendentium d(*omi*)ni Francisci'. It refers to Francesco di Pazzino Pazzi (d. 1341) and Simone di Ranieri Pazzi (d. 1343) who are given by Litta (*Famiglie celebri italiane*, viii, tav. 2, 3) as consanguinei, not father and son as claimed by Burger (p. 75). The formula of the inscription may mean that the tomb was erected either before the death of Francesco in 1341 or by Francesco's sons after the death of Simone in 1343. The second explanation is perhaps preferable. The earliest instance so far known of virtue-figures as supports is probably Giovanni Pisano's tomb of Margaret of Brabant (d. 1311) formerly in San Francesco di Castelletto, Genoa, which was dismantled and partly destroyed at the beginning of the nineteenth century (see C. Marcenaro 'Per la tomba di Margherita di Brabante' in *Paragone*, xii, 1961, pp. 1–17; M. Seidel, 'Ein neu entdecktes Fragment des Genueser Grabmals der Königin Margarethe von Giovanni Pisano' in *Pantheon*, xxvi, 1968, pp. 335–51; D. D. Pincus, 'A hand by Antonio Rizzo and the Double Caritas scheme of the Tron tomb,' in *Art Bulletin*, li, 1969, p. 252, n. 27). For the tomb of Giovanni Cossa see G. C. Capaccio, *Antiquitates et historiae Campaniae Felicis* (originally published at Naples in 1604), ed. in Graevius, *Thesaurvs Antiquitatum et Historiarum Italiae*, ix, pt. 3, Leyden, 1723, col. 140, who gives the only copy of his epitaph: *Hic iacet corpus magnifici domini Ioannis Cossae de Ischa, militis prothontini, et cetera; Insule Procidae domini, qui obiit Ischae anno domini MCCCXCVII die IV Aug. V. Ind. cvivs anima requiescat in pace. Amen.* Baldassare paid 7 ducats annually to St. Peter's, Rome, for an anniversary for his soul on 4 August each year (Esch, 1972, p. 763, n. 178).

18. For the tomb see L. Filippini, *La scultura del trecento in Roma*, Turin, 1908, pp. 172–5.

19. See the documents printed in the article by Lazzarini cited in n. 33. S. Weber, *Die Entwickelung des Putto in der Plastik der Früh-Renaissance*, Heidelberg, 1898, is purely a study of the formal type.

20. Del Corazza, *Diario fiorentino*, ed. cit., p. 275, '*era uomo compresso, bruno*'. For the interpretation of *compresso* see F. Sacchetti, *Il Trecentonovelle*, Turin, 1970, ed. E. Faccioli, p. 37, n. 3–4. Aragonese emissary in a report of 1419 (printed in Fincke, iii, pp. 295–6).

21. Pierre Ameilh, 'Ordo Romanus XV' in Mabillon, *Musaeum Italicum*, ii, Paris, 1724, cap. 166, pp. 541–2.

22. Johannes Burckhardt, *Liber Notarum*, i, (ed. *R.I.S.*, vol. 32), pp. 14–17.

23. Del Migliore, *Firenze città nobilissima*, 1684, pp. 96–7.

24. Del Migliore, *op. cit.*, p. 95.

25. Cardinal Talleyrand de Périgord, printed by Duchesne, ii, p. 312.

26. Janson, pp. 63–4, 57–8. H. M. Caplow (*Michelozzo*, i, p. 127) interprets the reference in Michelozzo's 1427 *catasto* return to a debt of 5 florins due to Benedetto di Marco da Terrarossa *fornaciaio* for '*calcina e mattoni*' (lime and bricks) as indicating that Michelozzo did the casting. The text does not support her interpretation: compare Vespasiano da Bisticci, *Vite*, iii, 1893, p. 327: '*S'acconciò con uno fornaciaio che coceva calcina e mattoni et era il suo esercizio mettere fuoco nella fornace.*'

27. This is evident from his *portata* of 1427, in which he declares his real estate.

28. For Nanni di Miniato see Fabriczy, 'Nanni di Miniato' in *Jahrbuch der Königlich Preussischen Kunstsammlungen*, xxvii, 1906, Beiheft, pp. 70–83, especially the appendix of documents.

29. Fabriczy, *op. cit.*, p. 77.

30. For Pagno di Lapo see Fabriczy, 'Pagno di Lapo Portigiani', in *Jahrbuch der Königlich Preussischen Kunstsammlungen*, xxiv, 1903, Beiheft, pp. 119–36; H. W. Janson, 'Two problems in Florentine Renaissance Sculpture', in *Art Bulletin*, xxiv, 1942, pp. 326–9.

31. P. Bacci, *Jacopo della Quercia, nuovi documenti*, Siena, 1929, pp. 174, 211, Janson, p. 62.

32. For Doge Tommaso Mocenigo and the posthumous erection of his tomb see A. da Mosto, *I dogi di Venezia*, Milan, 1960, p. 161. For the tomb itself see P. Paoletti, *L'architettura e la scultura del rinascimento in Venezia*, 1893, p. 76, i, pl. 22; M. Reymond, 'La tomba di Onofrio Strozzi nella chiesa della Trinità in Firenze', in *L'Arte*, vi, 1903, p. 14; Venturi, *Storia*, vi, 1908, p. 222, fig. 125; G. Fiocco, 'I Lamberti a Venezia – II, Pietro di Niccolò Lamberti', in *Dedalo*, viii, 1927–8, pp. 356–63; L. Planiscig, 'Die Bildhauer Venedigs in der ersten Hälfte des Quattrocento', in *Vienna Jahrbuch*, n.s. iv, 1930, pp. 62–6; Janson, p. 62.

33. The documents concerning the Fulgosio tomb are published by V. Lazzarini, 'Il mausoleo di Raffaelo Fulgosio nella Basilica del Santo', in *Archivio Veneto-Tridentino*, iv, 1923, pp. 147–53, and E. Rigoni, 'Notizie di scultori toscani a Padova nella prima metà del quattrocento', in *Archivio Veneto*, ser. 5, vi, 1929, pp. 121, 130. See also Gonzati, *La basilica di S. Antonio di Padova*, ii, Padua, 1853, pp. 119–21; Venturi, *Storia*, vi, 1908, pp. 226, 228; Fiocco, *art. cit.*, in *Dedalo*, viii, 1927–8, pp. 371–4; Planiscig, *art. cit.*, in *Vienna Jahrbuch*, n.s. iv, 1930, pp. 68–70, figs. 59–66.

34. For the Cossa tomb see, besides the literature already cited, Semper, *Donatello, seine Zeit und seine Schule*, Vienna, 1875, reg. 61, p. 281; A. Schmarsow, *Donatello*, Breslau, 1886, pp. 24–5; H. Semper, *Donatellos Leben und Werke*, Innsbruck, 1887, pp. 42–5; H. von Tschudi, *Donatello e la critica moderna*, Turin, 1887, pp. 11–12; W. Pastor, *Donatello*, Giessen, 1892, pp. 51–5; W. von Bode, *Denkmäler der Renaissance-Sculptur Toscanas*, Munich, 1892–1905, pp. 17–18; *id.*, *Florentiner Bildhauer der Renaissance*, Berlin, 1902, pp. 59–62; M. Reymond, *La sculpture florentine; première moitié du XVe siècle*, Florence, 1898, pp. 98–9, 156–7; Wolff, 1900, pp. 20–31; Lord Balcarres, *Donatello*, London, 1903, pp. 72–5; Burger, 1904, pp. 89–113, including an interesting essay on the influence of the tomb; Venturi, *Storia*, vi, 1908, pp. 258–60; P. Schubring, *Donatello*, Stuttgart and Leipzig, 1907, p. xxiii, pl. 24–6, pp. 194–5; M. Cruttwell, *Donatello*, London, 1911, pp. 54–6; Papini, in *Bollettino d'Arte*, ix, 1915, pp. 278–80; A. Colasanti, *Donatello*, Rome, 1931, pp. 46–7, 53–4; H. Kauffmann, *Donatello*, Berlin, 1935, pp. 96–7, 228, n. 313; Morisani, 1951, pp. 23–4, 87; Janson, 1963, pp. 59–64; L. Grassi, *Tutta la scultura di Donatello*, Milan, 1963, pp. 24, 71–2; Longhurst, O.12. The latest study of the tomb is in the thesis by H. M. Caplow, *Michelozzo*, i, New York and London, 1977, pp. 98–140. Like previous scholars, she has missed the implications of Pope Martin's complaint to the Signoria for the history and design of the tomb. This in turn has affected the value of the attributions she makes of sections of the tomb to different hands.

NOTES TO CHAPTER III

1. The best general account of Brancaccio's life is the short biography by D. Girgensohn in *Dizionario biografico degli italiani*, xvii, 1971, pp. 797–9, which appeared when my own researches were nearly completed. The brief article by M-Th. Didier, in Meyer & Cauwenbergh, *Dictionnaire d'histoire et de géographie ecclésiastiques*, x, 1938, pp. 387–90, is valueless. The earlier article by P. Mazio, 'Di Rinaldo Brancaccio Cardinale e di Onorato I Conte di Fondi', in *Il Saggiatore*, iv, 1845, pp. 296–314, 321–4, constantly cited by art-historians as the only general study of Brancaccio, contains few facts in many words. There are brief accounts of the Brancacci in general histories of Neapolitan families, e.g. B. Candida Gonzaga, *Memorie delle famiglie nobili delle province meridionali d'Italia*, i, Naples, 1875, pp. 134–9. Fortunately, the branch to which the Cardinal belonged and the Cardinal himself were treated at great length in E. Ricca, *La nobiltà delle Due Sicilie*, v, Naples, 1879. Ricca's unaccountably neglected account of the Cardinal (pp. 528–61) prints a number of fundamental documents which have been completely overlooked. I have made much use of it in my account of the Cardinal's family and the Neapolitan side of his life. I spell his name Brancaccio in the singular, and Brancacci in the plural; this is the correct usage. Also useful is the standard early biography, written in the later decades of the sixteenth century, partly on the basis of family archives, by Ciacconius, *Vitae et res gestae Pontificum Romanorum et S.R.E. Cardinalium*, Rome, ed. of 1630, col. 992, no. 51. Ciacconius records the details given below of the Cardinal's physical appearance.

2. F. Bologna, *I Pittori alla Corte Angoina di Napoli 1266–1414*, Naples, 1969, pp. 142–3, n. 54. There has been a certain amount of confusion between the Brancacci chapel dedicated to San Andrea, and a chapel dedicated to the same saint founded by the wealthy banking family of Gattola. Ricca (*op. cit.*, p. 535) claims without evidence that the Gattola sold their chapel to the Brancacci: Bologna that the Gattola chapel was not a chapel in San Domenico at all but the small church of Sant' Andrea de' Gattoli founded in 1305 by Pietro Gattola. A document printed by Ricca (*loc. cit.*, n. 712) seems, nevertheless, to show that there was indeed a chapel of the Gattola dedicated to San Andrea in San Domenico during the fourteenth century, for it records a bequest made to it in 1385 by Perrona Gattola.

3. C. Foucard, 'Descrizione della città di Napoli e statistica del Regno nel 1444', in *Archivio storico per le province napoletane*, ii, 1877, p. 732. The literature of the *Seggi*, much of it taken up with controversy about their origins and development, is enormous. Fundamental is the book of the seventeenth century antiquary Cammillo Tutini, *Dell' origine e fundazion de' Seggi di Napoli*. I have used the edition of 1754. Cf. also M. Schipa, 'Contese sociali napoletane', in *Archivio storico per le province napoletane*, xxxii, 1907, pp. 314–77.

4. R. degli Albizzi, *Commissioni*, ed. C. Guasti, ii, pp. 215–16. See also n. 1.

5. These events are narrated in all histories of Naples and the Papacy. A modern summary with previous literature is in Società Editrice Storia di Napoli, *Storia di Napoli*, iii, Naples, 1969. The section on religious history by D. Ambrasi and the narrative section by C. de Frede should both be consulted. The main contemporary narrative source is the *De Schismate* of Dietrich von Nieheim, vivid, prejudiced and inaccurate; it should be consulted in G. Erler's admirable edition of 1890.

6. For Papal acolytes see A. B. Meehan, in *The Catholic Encyclopaedia*, i, 1907, pp. 106–8.

7. Lucca, R. Archivio di Stato, *Regesti*, ii, *Carteggio degli Anziani*, 1903, p. 247. For Carlo see Esch in *Dizionario biografico degli italiani*, xiii, 1971, pp. 767–9.

8. *Op. cit.*, pp. 80–1.

9. Eubel, *Hierarchia Catholica medii aevi*, i, 1913, p. 25; F. Cantelori, *Elenchvs Eminentiss.ᵐ & Reverendiss.ᵐ S.R.E. Cardinalivm ab anno 1294 ad annum 1430*, Rome, 1641, pp. 118–22.

10. See Rubric XXX of the *Liber Caeremonialis* of *c.* 1410 (Vat. 4736) printed in J. B. Gattico, *Acta Selecta Caeremonialia Sanctae Romanae Ecclesiae*, Rome, 1753, p. 249.

11. Finke, 'Eine Papstkronik des XV Jahrhunderts', in *Römische Quartalschrift*, iv, 1890, p. 361.

12. The indispensable study of cardinals in the fourteenth century is G. Mollat, 'Contribution à l'histoire du Sacré Collège de Clément V à Eugène IV', in *Revue d'histoire ecclésiastique*, xlvi, pt. I, 1951, pp. 22–112; pt. II, pp. 566–94.

13. St. Antonino, *Tertia pars summae majoris*, tit. XXI, *De statu cardinalium*. The verse is from the Canticle of Anna.

14. Mollat, *op. cit.*, i, pp. 80–93. The skeleton, but not the flesh of what follows is taken from this admirable article.

15. Mazio, *op. cit.* in n. 1; G. Caetani, *Domus Caetana*, i, pt. I, San Casciano, 1927, p. 322; L. Ermini, *Onorato I Caetani Conte di Fondi e lo Scisma di Occidente*, Rome, 1938, pp. 91 ff.; B. Amante and R. Bianchi, *Memorie storiche e statutarie . . . di Fondi in Campania*, Rome, 1903, pp. 123–5.

16. Bliss and Twemlow, *Papal Letters*, vii, 1906, p. 480 (in London, Public Record Office, *Calendar of entries in the Papal Registers relating to Great Britain and Ireland*).

17. Bliss and Twemlow, *vol. cit.*, p. 505.

18. See Lisini, 'Papa Gregorio XII e i senesi', in *Rassegna Nazionale*, xci, 1896, p. 282.

19. Bliss and Twemlow, *op. cit.*, iv, 1902, pp. 378–9. John was canonised as St. John of Bridlington.

20. *De officialibus singulorum cardinalium S.R.E.*, printed in Gattico, *op. cit.*, p. 274; Mollat, pp. 50–8.

21. Vespasiano da Bisticci, *Vite di uomini illustri del secolo XV*, ed. P. D'Ancona and E. Aeschlimann, Milan, 1951, pp. 70–2, 78–91.

22. See for instance Poggio, *Facetiae*, ed. Liseux, 1879, no. 228.

23. By P. Meller (see n. 28).

24. Eubel, *Hierarchia*, i, pp. 25, 497; D. Taccone-Gallucci, *Monografia della patriarcale basilica di Santa Maria Maggiore*, Rome, 1911, p. 56. P. Fedele, 'I capitoli della pace fra re Ladislao e Giovanni XXIII', in *Archivio storico per le province napoletane*, xxx, 1905, pp. 184–5, 190–1, 195, 209.

25. Hardt, *Rerum Concilii Oecumenici Constantientis*, iv, p. 1489 (on 21 November); Hardt, *vol. cit.*, p. 1555.

26. L. Frati, 'Papa Martino V e il "Diario" di Cambio Cantelmi', in *Archivio storico italiano*, ser. 5, xlviii, 1911, p. 134; *Cronicon Fratris Hieronymi de Forlivio*, ed. A. Pasini (*R.I.S.*, xix, pt. 5), Bologna, 1931, pp. 30–1; Lucca, R. Archivio di Stato, *Regesti*, iii, pt. 2, *Carteggio di Ser Guido Manfredi*, p. 23.

27. Del Corazza, *Diario, cit.*, in *Archivio storico italiano*, ser. 5, xiv, 1894, p. 274; *Carteggio di Ser Guido Manfredi cit.*, p. 76, letter of 19 April 1419 from Giovanni Bindi.

28. Meller, 'La cappella Brancacci: problemi ritrattistici ed iconografici' in *Acropoli*, i, 1960–1, pp. 273–6. Is the costume worn by the rich man really that of a cardinal? The index to Guasti's edition of Rinaldo degli Albizzi's *Commissioni* mistakenly refers many passages to Tommaso rather than to Rainaldo Brancaccio.

29. *Diario, ed. cit.*

30. Mittarelli and Costadoni, *Annales Camaldulenses*, vi, Venice, 1761, p. 166; ix, 1773, p. 98.

31. G. A. Summonte, *Historia della città e regno di Napoli*, pt. II, Naples, 1601 (1599), pp. 540–1, dating the revival to 1407. For the date of 1420 see Ambrasi, in *Storia di Napoli cit.*, iii, 1969, pp. 539–40, 571 n. 15, citing S. D'Aloe, *Storia dell' Augustissima Compagnia della Disciplina della Santa Croce*, Naples, 1882.

32. Platina, life of Martin in *Vitae Pontificum* (many eds.); for the programme of visitation and repair Cantelori, *Martini Quinti vita*, in same vol. as *Elenchus*, Rome, 1641, p. 17.

33. Albizzi, *Commissioni*, i, pp. 364–5; ii, passim.

34. Printed as Appendix B.

35. Onofrio Panvinio, *De Praecipvis Vrbis Romae sanctioribusque basilicis*, Rome, 1570, p. 67, mentions this palace: '*Propinquum eius palatium ruinosum, nostro tempore qui illum incoluit reparavit Ioannes Cardinalis Moronus episcopus Portuensis, olim eius basilicae praesbyter Cardinalis*'.

36. Niccolò de Senatibus is mentioned as his chaplain in *Carteggio di Ser Guido Manfredi* (R. Archivio di Stato, Lucca, *Regesti*, iii, pt. 2), Pescia, 1933, p. 201.

37. For the members of Brancaccio's family see Ricca, *Nobiltà delle due Sicilie*, v, p. 604 (Giovanello, who seems later to have abandoned an ecclesiastical career and married); pp. 605–6 (Paolo), p. 604 (Fusco).

38. I make this identification from M. Parascandola, *Cenni storici intorno alla città ed isola di Procida*, Naples, 1892, pp. 32–3, who records Giovanni Carlo as the brother of Michele Cossa, the nephew of John XXIII and as '*Abbate di Procida e di S. Maria in Positano*'.

39. See Iris Origo, *The Merchant of Prato*, London, 1957, pp. 291–2. Dietrich von Nieheim, *De Schismate*, p. 72, praises the *vina greca* of Somma, outside Naples.

40. D'Aiello held the office of *clericus camerae apostolicae* from 16 September 1415 and that of *consiliarius* from 20 September 1417 (Eubel, p. 362). Urban VI had made him Bishop of Marsi in 1385; from Marsi he was translated to Nicastro in 1399 and from Nicastro to Sessa in 1418. See also Finke, iv, p. 229.

41. Mollat, 'Le Sacré Collège', pp. 64–72.

42. Girgensohn, *op. cit.*, p. 798 (see n. 1 to this chapter).

43. P. M. Baumgarten, *Untersuchungen und Urkunden über die Camera Collegii für die Zeit von 1295 bis 1437*, Leipzig, 1898, pp. 189, 232–3, 201–2; H. von Sauerland, *Urkunden und Regesten*, vi, Bonn, 1912, p. 296, no. 695; vii, p. 153, no. 384: G. Tellenbach, *Repertorium Germanicum*, ii, 1933, col. 1010–13; Theiner, *Vet. mon. hist. Hung. ill.*, ii, 1859, p. 192, no. 351; U. Kühne,

Repertorium Germanicum, iii, 1935, col. 324; Baix, *La Chambre Apostolique et les 'Libri Annatarum' de Martin V*, i, Brussels and Rome, pp. xcviii, 194, no. 521; J. de Theux de Montjardin, *Le Chapitre de Saint-Lambert*, ii, Brussels, 1871, pp. 156–7.

44. Bliss and Twemlow, *Papal Letters*, iv, pp. 383–4; pp. 468–9; p. 480; p. 504; *id.*, v, p. 287; *id.*, vi, pp. 239–40, 411, 474.

45. Mollat, *loc. cit.* For an amusing instance of the Cardinal dunning for his dues from a benefice see R. Archivio di Stato, Lucca, *Regesti*, iii, pt. 2, Pescia, 1933, pp. 70, 201, pp. 64, 74–5, 76, 80, pp. 120–1; pp. 160, 173, 182; *Registi*, iii, pt. i, pp. 489, 128.

46. Baumgarten, *op. cit.*, p. 185.

47. Ricca, *op. cit.*, pp. 533–4. C. Franchi, *Difesa dell' Illustre Piazza di Nido per Lo Padronato Laicale della Chiesa, ed Ospedale di S. Angelo* (1746), pp. xxviii–ix: G. Parente, *Origini e vicende ecclesiastiche della città di Aversa*, ii, Naples, 1858, p. 584.

48. For San Domenico see Ambrasi in *Storia di Napoli*, iii, pp. 491–8; A. Venditti, 'Urbanistica e architettura angoina', in *Storia cit.*, pp. 731–8. For Brancaccio's protectorate of the Dominicans see Orlandi, *Necrologio di S. Maria Novella*, ii, Florence, 1955, p. 178.

49. Pietro Caracciolo Cassano was in fact promoted to Aversa on 30 September 1427 (Eubel). C. Franchi, *Difesa*, p. xxx; Ricca, *Nobiltà*, v, p. 542.

50. Giuseppe Sigismondo, *Descrizione della città di Napoli*, ii, Naples, 1788, pp. 41 ff.; Ricca, *loc. cit.*, pp. 542–3.

51. Finke, *Acta Concilii Constanciencis*, ii, p. 657.

52. Mollat, pp. 77–9; B. Guillemain, *La cour pontificale d'Avignon 1309–76: étude d'une société*, Paris, 1966, pp. 215–16.

53. Pastor, i, pp. 243–4.

54. C. Franchi, *Difesa*, p. xlvii.

55. Printed in full by Ricca, *op. cit.*, pp. 543–45.

56. Franchi, *op. cit.*, pp. xxx–xxxi. A Paolo Brancaccio, nicknamed Gualerella, sold property in this year to the two proctors for the endowment and in the years that followed sold them more. It does not appear whether he was the same person as the Cardinal's nephew (Franchi, pp. lxxv–vi).

57. For Artusio Pappacoda and his family see B. Capasso 'Il Palazzo di Fabrizio Colonna a Mezzocannone . . . II: il palazzo nel sec. xv – I Pappacoda e gli Orsini,' in *Napoli Nobilissima*, iii, pp. 33–4; Ammirato, *Delle famiglie nobili napoletane Parte Seconda*, Florence, 1651, p. 287.

58. In his bull Martin uses the term *oratorium* for the chapel: this meant a private as opposed to a parochial foundation (Franchi, p. lxxiii).

59. For the original document see Ricca, *op. cit.*, pp. 547–51.

60. Printed as Appendix B.

61. The identification was made by Franchi in 1746. For San Giovanni dei Pappacoda see N. del Pezzo, 'La cappella di San Giovanni dei Pappacoda', in *Napoli Nobilissima*, vii, 1898, pp. 185–90: C. D'Engenio Caracciolo, *Napoli Sacra*, Naples, 1624, p. 257.

62. Giuseppe Sigismondo, *Descrizione . . . di Napoli*, ii, 1788, p. 204; F. Nicolini, *L'arte napoletana del rinascimento e la lettera di Pietro Summonte a Marcontonio Michiel*, Naples, 1925, p. 160. Nicolini (pp. 166–71) suggests that they may have been derived from Giotto's Apocalypse cycle in the Oratorio delle Clarisse in Santa Chiara, and were perhaps painted by Leonardo di Maestro Andrea di Sulmona, whom King Ladislaus appointed a member of his household on 10 May 1407. However, the same document also names three other painters and among so many names it is idle to make a choice of Messer Artusio's artist.

63. C. D'Engenio Caracciolo, *Napoli Sacra*, Naples, 1624, p. 259. G. Ceci, 'Il Palazzo Penna', in *Napoli Nobilissima*, iii, 1894, pp. 83–6; F. Bologna, *op. cit.*, p. 349.

64. Eubel, i, p. 34. Ardicino had taken an important part in the process against Gregory and Benedict at the Council of Pisa (Vincke, 'Acta Concilii Pisani', in *Römische Quartalschrift*, xlvi, 1938, p. 94).

65. R. de Roover, *Il Banco Medici dalle origini al declino*, Florence, 1970, pp. 71–2.

66. Ricca, *Nobiltà*, v, pp. 541–2, citing Naples, Archivio di Stato, *Repertorio delle Pergamene della Università e della città di Aversa*, p. 43, no. xxix.

67. L. Bertalot, 'Zwölf Briefe des Ambrogio Traversari', in *Römische Quartalschrift*, xxix, 1915, pp. 103*–5*.

68. Cod. Vat. Lat. 12123, c. 284', cit. by D. Girgensohn, in *Dizionario biografico degli italiani*, xiii, pp. 798–9.

69. Pierre Ameilh, *Ordo Romanus XV*, in Mabillon, *Musaeum italicum*, Paris, 1724, pp. 541–3, cap. 166. Different ceremonies naturally varied in details. Compare the various accounts of the ceremony evidently noted at different times, in Ameilh and Mollat, 'Le Sacré Collège', pp. 587–91. But the principal elements are clear.

NOTES TO CHAPTER IV

1. Duchesne, ii, pp. 359, 365, 382–3, 424, 542.

2. Duchesne, ii, pp. 617, 501. On the tombs of fourteenth-century cardinals see G. Mollat, 'Contribution à l'histoire du Sacré Collège', in *Revue d'histoire ecclésiastique*, xlvi, 1941, pp. 567–94.

3. For the Fieschi tomb (Longhurst C12) a Cosmatesque work, see Venturi, *Storia*, iii, 1904, p. 894, fig. 70; Burger, p. 15; R. Thynne, *The Churches of Rome*, 1924, pp. 56–7. The most recent discussion of the tomb of Guillaume de Braye is in A. M. Romanini, *Arnolfo di Cambio e lo 'stil novo' del gotico italiano*, Milan, 1969, pp. 23–56. For the epitaph see p. 53, n. 46.

4. J. Gardner, 'The tomb of Cardinal Anni-

baldi by Arnolfo di Cambio', in *Burlington Magazine*, cxiv, 1972, pp. 136–41.

5. For the Petroni tomb (Longhurst D3) see in addition to the standard literature on Tino di Camaino, J. Bignami-Odier, 'Le testament du Cardinal Richard Petroni (25 janvier 1314)', in *Studies in Italian mediaeval history presented to Miss E. M. Jamison* (Papers of the British School at Rome, xxiv, 1956, pp. 142–57). See p. 153 for the clause of his will ordering his body to be taken to Siena and buried 'in ipsius ecclesie pariete'.

6. It should be said that a number of important *trecento* tombs have been moved and partly destroyed; so that their form when complete is a matter for conjecture.

7. For the tomb of Cardinal Carbone see L. Parascandolo, *Memorie storiche – critiche – diplomatiche della Chiesa di Napoli*, iv, 1851, pp. 29–30; L. de la Ville sur Yllon, 'Le navate minori del Duomo', in *Napoli Nobilissima*, v, 1896, pp. 82–3; R. Filangieri di Candida, 'La scultura in Napoli nei primi albori del Rinascimento', in *Napoli Nobilissima*, n.s., i, 1920, p. 66. Parascandolo quotes a letter of 11 July 1406, preserved among the acts of Archbishop Annibale di Capoa (p. 173), referring to a convention concerning the chapel passed between the Chiesa Arcivescovile and Masone Carbone and others of the Carbone family. This states that the Cardinal had been buried in his chapel in 1405.

8. For the Minutolo tomb see S. Fraschetti, 'Il monumento di Arrigo Minutolo' in *Napoli Nobilissima*, xi (n.s., i), 1902, pp. 66–7. There is some reason to think that the work was completed by March 1405 (cf. p. 271, n. 20).

9. These instructions are printed by R. de Roover, *Il banco Medici dalle origini al declino (1397–1494)*, Florence, 1970, pp. 556–9.

10. For Dwerg, see Pastor, *The History of the Popes*, i, 1899, pp. 243–4, and the scoffing comments of De Roover (*op. cit.*, pp. 301–2) on Pastor's rhapsody.

11. Luigi Aldomorisco's wife was named Isabella Brancaccio. For the Aldomorisco tomb see the documents printed in G. Filangieri,

Documenti per la storia le arti e le industrie della Provincie Napoletane, ii, Naples, 1884, pp. 98–103, and O. Ferrari, 'Per la conoscenza della scultura del primo quattrocento a Napoli', in *Bollettino d'Arte*, xxxix, 1954, pp. 17–24. For Baboccio see Ferrari's article, and also his article in *Dizionario biografico degli italiani*, Rome, 1962, s.v., with full bibliography.

12. James H. Beck, *Jacopo della Quercia e il portale di San Petronio a Bologna*, Bologna, 1970, p. 14.

13. For the *catasto* return see Fabriczy, p. 62. For the dates of Donatello's presence in Pisa see L. Tanfani Centofanti, *Donatello in Pisa* (1878); *id.*, *Notizie di artisti*, Pisa, 1897, pp. 176–81 which must be read together with Janson, pp. 89–90, especially his n. 4 which corrects previous errors of dating arising from ignorance of the Pisan style. For the identification of the workshop see B. Casini, *Il catasto di Pisa del 1428–9*, Pisa, 1964, pp. 72–3, Nos. 312, 313, 316. The name is given in Michelozzo's *castasto* return (as printed by Fabriczy) as 'Bartolommeo dallanaina'. The name in this form does not appear in the Pisan *catasto* returns and it is clearly the same as da Lavaiano, as study of the indices to Casini, *op. cit.*, s.v. Bartolommeo, reveals. The identification is also confirmed by the connection with Andrea de' Bardi. Lavaiano is between Pisa and Lucca. For the position of San Sepolcro and San Cristofano see the seventeenth-century plan of Pisa reproduced from a nineteenth-century engraving with key by Casini (facing p. 1). For Andrea de' Bardi, see De Roover, *op. cit.*, pp. 56–7.

14. Gaye, *Carteggio d'artisti*, i, p. 118 n.: a corrected figure and reading in De Roover, *op. cit.*, p. 329 n.: '*Michelozzo e Donatello intagliatori, per una sepultura del Cardinale Branchacci, carta 7, fiorini 188 s. 1 d. 11 a fior.*'

15. The first mention of the tomb in the printed topographical literature of Naples occurs in Pietro di Stefano, *Descrittione de i lvoghi sacri della città di Napoli et Epitaphii scelti che in quelle si ritrovano*, 1560, Naples, f. 33r and verso: '*Dentro detta Chiesa ui è un bello sepolcro di marmo, dove sta il mortale di detto Cardinale senza alcun Epitaphio.*' The bibliography of the secondary literature on the Brancaccio tomb is as follows:

L. Cicognara, *Storia della scultura dal suo risorgimento in Italia*, 2nd ed., iv, Prato, 1823, pp. 117–18. '*E come arida e secca, e stentata si dirà la maniera di questo classico autore, allorchè osservando in Napoli le belle figure che sostengono a S. Angelo in Nido l'arca sepolcrale del cardinale Rinaldo di Brancacci, si gitterà poi lo sguardo sul bassorilievo nella faccia del sarcofago, il quale è scolpito in marmo con tanto fuoco d'immaginazione che più a tocco di pennello rapido e magistrale, che a lento, e tedioso meccanismo di ferri direbbesi appartenere.*' H. W. Schulz, *Denkmäler der Kunst des Mittelalters in Unteritalien*, iii, 1860, pp. 98–9; Bode, in Jacob Burckhardt, *Der Cicerone*, 4th ed., ii, Leipzig, 1879, p. 356 (recognising the lack of finish of the figures). A. Schmarsow, *Donatello*, 1886, p. 26; Bode in *J.P.K.*, xxii, 1901, p. 24, n. 1; H. Semper, *Donatellos Leben und Werke*, Innsbruck, 1887, pp. 45–9; M. Reymond, *La sculpture florentine: première moitié du XVᵉ siècle*, Florence, 1898, pp. 100–1, 157; P. Schubring, *Das italienische Grabmal der Frührenaissance*, 1904, p. 8, and *Donatello*, 1907, pp. xxvi, 196; Wolff, 1900, pp. 31–40; Bode, *Florentiner Bildhauer der Renaissance*, 1902, pp. 57–89; Balcarres, *Donatello*, London, 1903, pp. 77–82; C. von Fabriczy, 'Recherches nouvelles sur Donatello, Masaccio et Vellano', in *G.B.A.*, ser. 3, viii, 1892, pp. 328–9; Burger, 1904, pp. 114–20; Venturi, *Storia*, vi, 1908, pp. 260–4, figs. 114–15, viii, 1923, pt. 1, pp. 282–3; M. Cruttwell, *Donatello*, London, 1911, pp. 56–8; A. Colasanti, *Donatello*, Rome, 1931, p. 53; H. Kauffmann, *Donatello*, Berlin, 1935, pp. 42–3, 49–50. Valentiner, 'Donatello and Ghiberti' in *Art Quarterly*, iii, 1940, p. 203; Morisani, 1951, pp. 25–6, 87–8; Janson, 1963, pp. 88–92; L. Grassi, *Tutta la scultura di Donatello*, Milan, 1963, p. 72; V. Martinelli, 'La "compagnia" di Donatello e di Michelozzo e la sepultura del Brancacci a Napoli' in *Commentari*, xiv, 1963, pp. 211–26; *id.*, 'Per una rilettura del monumento Brancacci', in *Napoli Nobilissima*, n.s., iv, 1964, pp. 3–11; R. di Stefano, 'La Chiesa di S. Angelo e il Seggio di Nido', *ib.*, pp. 12–21. O. Morisani, 'Il monumento Brancacci nell' ambiente napoletano del Quattrocento' in Instituto Nazionale di Studi sul Rinascimento, *Donatello e il suo tempo*, Florence, 1968, pp. 207–13. The latest study of the tomb is by H. M. Caplow, *Michelozzo*, i, New York and London, 1977, pp. 141–209. For Sant' Angelo a Nido see R. di Stefano, 'La chiesa di S. Angelo a Nido e il

Seggio di Nido', in *Napoli Nobilissima*, n.s. iv, 1964–5, pp. 12–21. The church is naturally mentioned in the guide-book literature of Naples.

16. There is no reference to San Bacolo in the Cardinal's will. For his supposed relationship to the Brancacci see Ricca, *La nobiltà delle due Sicilie*, v, pp. 116–29.

17. For these tiles, said to have come from the chapel in which the monument now stands, see G. Tesorone, 'A proposito dei pavimenti maiolicati del XV e XVI secolo delle chiese napoletane,' in *Napoli Nobilissima*, x, 1901, pp. 117, 122. A date *c.* 1430 is persistently advocated for them, on the assumption that they were laid down shortly after Sant' Angelo a Nido was erected (see e.g. G. Donatone, *Maioliche napoletane della Spezieria Aragonese di Castelnuovo*, Naples, 1970, p. 30, fig. 64). But the costume of the female busts indicates a date *c.* 1470 at the earliest, and the shaped tiles relate to others of this date, e.g. a tile from the pavement of the palace of Diomede Carafa in Maddaloni, dated by Donatone (*op. cit.*, fig. 54) after 1466. Moreover, what we know of the early history of Sant' Angelo indicates that there was no money *c.* 1430 for an expensive pavement of maiolica tiles.

18. For these two portals see G. Cosenza, 'Battenti e decorazione marmorea di antiche porte esistenti in Napoli', in *Napoli Nobilissima*, ix, 1900, pp. 51–2.

19. See bibliography in n. 15. According to the seventeenth-century antiquary C. Tutini, *Dell' origine e fundazion de' Seggi di Napoli*, Naples, ed. of 1754, pp. 49, 134–6, the initiative in re-building the *seggi* with greater splendour was taken by Montagna in 1409, followed by Capuana in 1453, and by Nido in 1476 (completed 1507). He says that the first Seggio of Nido was on a site opposite the Gesù where a house of the Afflitto family had once stood.

20. Carlo Celano, *Delle notitie del bello, dell' antico, e del curioso della città di Napoli*, iii (*Giornata terza*), Naples, 1692, pp. 147–55. From D'Engenio Carracciolo (*Napoli Sacra*, 1624, pp. 260–1) we know that the Marco da Siena altarpiece already stood on the high altar in 1624: '*Vedesi nell' Altar maggior della presente Chiesa la*

tauola oue'è dipinto S. Michele Archangelo, chi di sotto tiene il Demonio conculcato di eccelente e rara pittura, la qual fù fatta da Marco da Siena.' From his words we can deduce that there had been some remodelling of the church during the sixteenth century. Other descriptions of the church in later guide-books (e.g. Pompeo Sarnelli, *Guida de' Forestieri . . . della Regal Città di Napoli*, Naples, 1685, pp. 196–7, and Celano, *loc. cit.*) confirm that the presence of Marco da Siena's painting implies that the tomb had been moved to its present position before 1624.

21. Di Stefano, *loc. cit.* in n. 15. He is unlikely to have been mistaken on such a point, as his book is a collection of epitaphs.

22. Cesare d'Engenio Caracciolo, *Napoli Sacra*, Naples, 1624, pp. 260–1: '*senza epitaffio alcuno, si ben oggi dalla sua famiglia è stato posto il seguente epitaffio, come diremo. . . .*'

23. According to Carlo Franchi, *Difesa dell' Illustre Piazza di Nido*, Naples (1746), pp. lxxiii, lxx, Sant' Angelo is described by the Cardinal and his contemporaries as a *cappella* or *oratorium*, not as an *ecclesia*, the term used for it in the epitaph, but he notes (p. lxx) that it is referred to as an *ecclesia* in documents of 20 and 26 October 1428.

24. Some late nineteenth- and early twentieth-century scholars seem to have recognised the difficulty, but did little to solve it by suggesting that the three figures represent the three Fates, e.g. Balcarres and Schubring.

25. For Cristoforo Caetani and his tomb see G. Caetani, *Domvs Caetana*, i, pt. ii, Sancasciano, 1927, pp. 48–50, who says that it was erected by his son and successor Onorato II (d. 1491) in the Duomo (San Pietro) of Fondi. See also O. Ferrari, *art. cit.* in *Bollettino d'Arte*, xxxix, 1954, pp. 22, 24; B. Amante and R. Bianchi, *Memorie storiche e statutarie del ducato, della contea e dell' episcopato di Fondi*, Rome, 1903, pp. 129–30, and Schulz, *Denkmäler*, ii, p. 133.

26. Burger, p. 75.

27. For this see J. Gage, 'Ghiberti's *Third Commentary* and its background', in *Apollo*, xcv, 1972, pp. 364–9.

28. *Ordo Romanus XV* (*Liber Petri Amelii Episcopi Senegalliensis de Caeremoniis S.R.E.*) in Mabillon, *Musaeum Italicum*, ii, Paris, 1724, pp. 541–3, cap. clxvi, *De exsequiis cardinalium*. See also p. 44.

29. For the Longhi tomb (Longhurst K22) see Venturi, *Storia*, iv, p. 616.

30. Burger also emphasises the dramatic conception of the tomb.

31. For these see C. Cecchelli, *I mosaici della basilica di S. Maria Maggiore*, Turin, 1956, pp. 278–93, tav. lxxvii–viii.

NOTES TO CHAPTER V

1. The best and most accessible exposition of medieval beliefs about Michael is in Jacobus a Voragine, *Legenda aurea*, ed. Graesse, 1890, pp. 642–53. For medieval hymns to Michael expressing devotion to him as the conductor of souls see F. J. Mone, *Hymni Latini Medii Aevi*, i, Freiburg, 1853, pp. 447–56. The extract from the Mass of the Angels is from the *Breviarium Romanum*, Paris, 1528. See also the office *In dedicatione Sancti Michaelis archangeli* (29 September). For the Baptist, see f. lxxv r.

2. Quoted by H. s' Jacob, *Idealism and Realism*, Leyden, 1954, p. 132.

3. From *Commendationes animarum*, in the *Breviarium Romanum*, Paris, 1528, ff. lxxxv and verso, lxxxvii.

4. For the doctrine of a particular judgement, see X. Le Bachelet, 'Benoit XII, constitution Benedictus Deus, émise par lui le 29 janvier 1336', in *Dictionnaire de théologie catholique*, ed. A. Vacant and E. Mangenot, ii, 1905, cols. 657–96, and J. Rivière, 'Jugement', *ib.*, vii, 1924–5, s.v.

5. The general works on the iconography of angels are of no help in this context.

6. See *Breviarium Romanum*, Paris, 1528, seventh day, lectio iii. The letter is printed in St.

Jerome, *Opera omnia*, in Migne, *P.L.*, xl, cols. 126–47. Its authenticity was first questioned by Erasmus.

7. Longhurst, F10.

8. For Santa Maria Maggiore see D. Taccone-Gallucci, *Monografia della Patriarcale Basilica di Santa Maria Maggiore*, Rome and Grottaferrata, 1911; E. Lavagnini and V. Moschini, *Santa Maria Maggiore*, Rome, s.d. (1924?); C. Cecchelli, *I mosaici della basilica di S. Maria Maggiore*, Turin, 1956.

9. For the provenance of this famous altarpiece see M. Davies, *Early Italian Schools* (National Gallery Cat.), 1961, p. 352 and L. Berti, *Masaccio*, London, 1967, p. 161, n. 288. The Santa Maria ad Nives panel is now in the Museo di Capodimonte, Naples.

10. Mistakenly identified by Cecchelli (tav. lxxvi) as St. Jerome explaining the scriptures.

11. See H. Thurston, S.J., *The Holy Year of Jubilee*, London, 1900, pp. 140, 197–206.

12. For the literature of the Minutolo tomb see p. 267, n. 8.

13. Published by G. Milanesi, *Documenti per la storia dell' arte senese*, ii, Siena, 1854, p. 134, doc. 94. Morisani (p. 26) rightly denies that this letter gives any foundation for assigning any part of the Siena font to Michelozzo.

14. Pietro di Stefano, *Descrittione*, 1560, f. 11v.

15. De Roover, *Il banco Medici*, pp. 296, 299.

16. An extract from this document is printed by Carlo Franchi, *Difesa dell' Illustre Piazza di Nido*, Naples (1746), p. lxvii: 6 July 1428, '*Giovanni, e Paolo Brancaccio militi Fratelli Germani, ed Eredi Testamentarj del Cardinale, consegnano a' Nobili della Piazza di Nido il Possesso dell' Ospedale, e della Cappella de' SS. Angelo, ed Andrea congiunta all' Ospedale medesimo. . . . Constitutis D. Joanello de Brancaciis, & D. Paulo de Brancacciis Militibus . . . assignaverunt, & corporaliter tradiderunt dictis Nobilibus quoddam Hospitale, cum quadam Cappellâ cum dicto Hospitali conjuncta, quae non est picta, nec est vitrum in fenestris,* *sub vocabulo SS. Angeli, & Andreae de novo constructa, & aedificata per ipsum Dominum Cardinalem.*' It is summarised by Ricca, *Nobiltà*, v, p. 557, from a copy of the original notarial act drawn up by Galeotto de Rainaldo preserved in the Archivio of the Amministrazione of Sant' Angelo a Nido, xvii, ff. 626–39. Caplow (*op. cit.*, p. 161) suggests that the tomb was set up by Nanni di Banco.

17. Franchi, *op. cit.*, p. lxxv.

18. A. di Costanzo, *Istoria del Regno di Napoli*, ed. of Milan, ii, 1805, p. 216. According to Pietro di Stefano, *Descrittione*, 1560, f. 33r and v, the hospital looked after persons sick with fever and maintained in his time nine priests and four deacons.

19. Franchi, *op. cit.*, p. lxvii.

20. This is the chapel containing the Cardinal's tomb (cf. pp. 84, 115). He had founded an altar to St. Anastasia (the saint of his titular church as cardinal) in it in 1402; hence the changed dedication (cf. L. Parascandolo, *Memorie storiche-critiche-diplomatiche della Chiesa di Napoli*, iv, Naples, 1851, pp. 24–8).

21. Vasari, *Le vite de piv eccelenti architetti, pittori, et scvltori italiani*, i, p. 342.

22. Celano, *Delle notitie. . . . della città di Napoli*, iii, 1692, pp. 147–55.

23. De' Dominici, *Vite de' pittori, scultori ed architetti napoletani*, i, Naples, 1742, pp. 60–3, 99–101. De' Dominici wrote the section on the church in his life of Colantonio in 1729.

24. For these and other discussions of the tomb see p. 268, n. 15.

25. Vasari, *Vite*, ed. Milanesi, ii, 1878, p. 432.

26. By Morisani; cf. also Janson, p. 75.

27. L. Tanfanti-Centofanti, *Notizie di artisti tratte dai documenti pisani*, Pisa, 1897, pp. 176–81.

28. Lorenzo Ghiberti, *I Commentari*, ed. O. Morisani, Naples, 1947, pp. 211–14.

29. See M. Reymond, 'L'arc mixtiligne florentin', in *Rivista d'Arte*, i, 1904, pp. 245–59; U. Procacci, 'Niccolò di Pietro Lamberti e Niccolò di Luca Spinelli d'Arezzo', in *Il Vasari*, i, 1927–8, pp. 300–16.

NOTES TO CHAPTER VI

1. *Leonardi Bruni Epistolarum Libri VIII*, ed. L. Mehus, ii, Florence, 1741, bk. 6, letter 5, pp. 45–8.

2. Printed as Appendix C, doc. 1. from M.S. Gaddi I, ff. 211v–213r in the Biblioteca Medicea-Laurenziana (Bandinius, *Catalogvs codicvm latinorvm Bibliothecae Medicae Laurentianae*, iv, 1777, p. 2). The scribe of the Virgil was Johann Hornsen of Münster (the colophon reads *Scriptus per manus Iohannis Hornsen Monasterien. familiaris domini G. DE MONTE-POLITIANO*). For Johann Hornsen of Münster, who worked for various patrons at the Curia of Pope Pius II in the early 1460s, including Corrado da Montepulciano (whose coat of arms appears in Vat. lat. 222), see J. Ruysschaert, 'Miniaturistes "romains" sous Pie II', in *Enea Silvio Piccolomini Papa Pio II*, ed. D. Maffei, Siena, 1968, p. 253, n. 44. A later ownership inscription and coat of arms on ff. 1–2 shows that it belonged in the late sixteenth or early seventeenth century to Guido de' Nobili of Montepulciano. Later still the manuscript came into the possession of the convent of San Francesco in Montepulciano, whence it was transferred to the Laurenziana together with the other surviving manuscripts of the convent's once rich library in August 1758. Corrado Bellarmino, a curial official, held the Arcipretura of Montepulciano from 1431 to 1458, and was later a canon of St. Peter's.

3. All celebrated humanists. Poggio and Cencio de' Rustici had been Bartolommeo's colleagues and intimate friends. Biondo was Flavio Biondo of Forlì, Carlo of Arezzo was Carlo Marsuppini, who succeeded Bruni as Chancellor of the Florentine Republic, and whose tomb by Desiderio da Settignano is in Santa Croce.

4. Note and letter are printed in Appendix C, doc. 1. The first editor of Aleotti's letters (*Hieronymi Aleotti Arretini Epistolae & Opuscula*, ed. G. M. Scarmalius, i, Arezzo, 1769, p. 26, n.b.) was already aware that the letter was probably an answer to Bruni's, but could not do more than record his suspicion that this was so.

5. Also a native of Arezzo. Bacci took a doctorate at Siena and later became a *clericus camerae*.

6. Printed by Scarmalius, *op. cit.*, pp. 27–9.

NOTES TO CHAPTER VII

1. The bibliography of Montepulciano is not large. By far the most useful book on the town is the edition of Spinello Benci's *Storia di Montepulciano* issued in 1968 by Dr. Ilio Calabresi and Dr. Piero Tiraboschi. This contains (i) a facsimile reprint of a copy of the 1646 edition of Benci's history which has important annotations added by a local historian in the early nineteenth century: (ii) a facsimile reprint of the article on Montepulciano in the famous *Dizionario geografico fisico storico della Toscana* by Emanuele Repetti (from vol. iii, Florence, 1839, pp. 464–92) and a reprint of Repetti's articles on places in the surrounding countryside: (iii) a series of appendices, a bibliography, and an annotated index which contains invaluable notes on the history, constitution and antiquities of Montepulciano. Other works are cited in the notes below.

2. Vasari, 'Vita di Andrea Sansovino' in *Vite*, ed. Milanesi, iv, 1879, p. 522. The head of the statue is still preserved in Palazzo Avignonesi (see E. Fumi, *Guida di Montepulciano e dei Bagni di Chianciano*, Montepulciano, 1894, p. 17; F. Caroti, *Guida turistica di Montepulciano*, Montepulciano, 1969, p. 44). An engraving of a head of Lars Porsenna with the inscription: *Porsenae Haetr: Regi. Politianae Civitatis Fvndatori. Andreas Sansovinus Sculpsit* forms the frontispiece to Benci's history of Montepulciano (see n. 1). Already in the early seventeenth century there was a tradition of a later foundation in 367 A.D. by a Roman senator named Zenobius (see

Thomas Dempster, *De Etruria Regali*, ed. Th. Coke, ii, Florence, 1724, p. 422). Dempster rejected both versions as legends. The problem is discussed by I. Calabresi, 'Le origini e il nome di Montepulciano' in Benci, *ed. cit.*, pp. 265–71.

3. George Dennis, *The Cities and Cemeteries of Etruria*, ed. of 1878, ii, pp. 368–73. A brief modern account of Etruscan antiquities with bibliography in G. A. Secchi Tarugi, *Guida di Montepulciano*, Milan, s.d.

4. For the definition of a Pieve see V. Lusini, 'I confini storici del vescovado di Siena' in *Bullettino Senese di Storia Patria*, v, 1898, p. 345, n. 1. The document of 1195 is printed by U. Pasqui, *Documenti per la storia della città di Arezzo*, ii, Florence, 1916, p. 32 ff. (*cit.* Calabresi, 'Le origini').

5. For the urban history of Montepulciano during the Middle Ages see I. Calabresi, 'Montepulciano e il suo territorio nel medio-evo' in Benci, *ed. cit.*, pp. 275–92.

6. R. Caggese, *Classi e comuni rurali nel Medioevo italiano*, 1907–9, ii, pp. 79, 158.

7. They are usually described as brothers, but Dr. Calabresi tells me that they were in fact cousins.

8. For the constitution of Montepulciano in the Middle Ages see I. Scimonelli, 'Intorno agli Statuti del Comune di Montepulciano nel Secolo XIV' in *Bullettino Senese di Storia Patria*, v, 1898, pp. 394–410; vi, 1899, pp. 466–82; vii, 1900, pp. 403–17 and the notes by Dr. I. Calabresi in the index to Benci, *ed. cit.* under *Domini Quinque, Consiglio, Priori* etc. and his general essay 'La legislazione statutaria di Montepulciano e il suo posto nella storia del diritto italiano' in Benci, *ed. cit.*, pp. 251–62.

9. The fullest modern account of the ecclesiastical history of Montepulciano is contained in (Don Idro Marcocci) *Per conoscere Montepulciano*, Camaiore, 1965. For some notes on the Arcipreti of Montepulciano see his p. 23.

10. Archivio di Stato, Florence, *Catasto 191, Vescovado d'Arezzo*, ff. 431v–442r.

11. Repetti, in Benci, *ed. cit.*, p. 181.

12. For Sant' Agnese Segni (*c.* 1274 or 1268–1317) see C. di Agresti and D. Valori, 'Agnese da Montepulciano', in Istituto Giovanni XXIII, *Bibliotheca Sanctorum*, i, Rome, 1961, col. 375–81. The first Dominican father who instructed her nuns was however from Orvieto.

13. For saffron in medieval Tuscany see Iris Origo, *The Merchant of Prato*, 1957, p. 289.

14. Documents cited by Repetti, pp. 188–9 in Benci, *ed. cit.*

15. I print his account of the Aragazzi family in Appendix C, doc. 2.

16. Archivio di Stato, Florence 81/I primo fasc. Ser Mino da Montepulciano (1303–31), f. 32v, 1303, ind. I, 23 September: '*vendiderunt*. . . . *Ciutio qui vocatur Ragazius quondam andree*. . . .' Document kindly communicated by Dr. I. Calabresi.

17. Ser Mino da Montepulciano (see previous note) f. 10 'Paulus Ragacj'.

18. All my information about Francesco, except where I cite other documents, is taken from his *catasto* return of 1429, printed as Appendix C, doc. 3.

19. Montepulciano, Archivio, *Liber Apodixarum et Exitus Comunis* (*Apodisse dei Priori 8*) unnumbered folio, '*francisco bartolomei oratori transmisso Senas ad magistrum honofrium Johannis ad procurandum quod ipse magister honofrius acceptaret offitium magistratus gramatice dicti Comunis in totum lire octo soldi decemocto*': entry for 'oratore' to Nove is on an earlier unnumbered leaf. For the payment regarding the Jews see same book, f. 422r: 30 July 1418, '*francisco bartholomei per più uarie e diverse spese e per uarie cagioni facte per lui per la difesa dela comune da ragione di Venturello ebreo ll. trecento dodici soldi dieci*'.

20. Montepulciano, Archivio, *Liber Apodixarum et Exitus Comunis* (*Apodisse dei Priori 8*), f. 427, 30 August 1418, '*francisco bartholomei vexillifero populi ac eius consociis dominis prioribus dictae comunis pro subsidio unius cene facte potestati duobus stanijs vini albi*. . . . *ll. vi*'. *Liber Reformationum* (*Deliberazioni 27*), f. 64, 25 November 1422, at meeting of the *Consiglio Generale* '*in sala magna novi palatii*' he speaks as '*Franciscus Bartholomei domini nucij vnus ex dictis consiliariis*'; *ib.*, f. 52v, 3 September 1422, election of '*Officiales super speculo*'; f. 56v, 29 October 1422, elected one of the three '*Regulatores gabellarum*' together with Giovanni di Bartolommeo di Naldino, his relative and later to be his executor (see below). *Liber Reformationum* (*1427–9*) *Reformagionj Di Ser Martino* (*Deliberazioni 29*), f. 20r, 6 December 1427 – '*Septimo quod pro bono utilitate et honore comunis franciscus bartholomei extractus in vexilliferum populi dicte terre possit et valeat ad eius libitum dictum ad officium introyre et intrare et usque ad finem exercere dato non adsit in principio quancumque veniet non obstanti reformatione in contrarium cui sit derogatum*'. The proposal was referred as custom required to the Consiglio (f. 21r) which gave its consent that same day (f. 22r). *Liber. Ref. cit.* (*Deliberazioni 29*), f. 116r, 21 May 1429: '*franciscus bartholomei dni nucij unus ex consiliariis dicti Consilij accedens ad aringeriam in dicto consilio*. . . .'

21. Montepulciano, Archivio, *Liber Ref.* (*Deliberazioni 29*), f. 45v, 15 April 1428, '*Franciscus bartholomei dni nucij*' one of names to be submitted '*pro Terteria S. Marie*': f. 47r, one of six elected same day; f .72v, 1 November 1428, '*per consilium redditum per Franciscum bartholomei unum ex Capitaneis partis guelfe*'; f. 73v, 2 November 1428.

22. Montepulciano, Archivio, *Liber Ref.* (*Deliberazioni 29*), f. 135r, 8 October 1429: proposal to the *Priori*, '*Quinta cum deus omnipotens ad se elegerit bonam memoriam Francisci Bartholomei dni nuccij de montepolitiano qui erat unus ex tribus operariis aedis et conventus fratrum predicatorum dicte terre Ideo prouideatur in loco suo ut consilio videbitur*'; f. 137v, 8 October 1429; '*Item eligerunt dicti M(agnifici) S(ignori) Priores et Vexilliferi populi dicte terre vigore auctoritatis eisdem ut S. date loco bone memorie francisci bartholomei dni nuccij operarij Conventus fratrum Predicatorum dicte terre Andream bonaventure pro tempore et cum ea auctoritate et balia quam habent eius consocii et habebat dictus franciscus.*'

23. Bartolommeo Aragazzi writing to Ambrogio Traversari on 21 January 1417 from St. Gall, says that Ambrogio is *'genitorique meo coniunctissimum in amore, in charitate in Christo'* (*Ambrosii Traversarii Generalis Camaldvlensium . . . Epistolae*, ed. Mehus, ii, Florence, 1769, Lib. xxiv, Epist. 9, col. 983).

24. For these two confraternities see (Don Idro Marcocci) *Per conoscere Montepulciano*, 1965, pp. 109–10, 107–8.

25. See his *catasto* return, printed as Appendix C, doc. 3. For the reading of a pious merchant in late fourteenth century Tuscany see I. Origo, *The Merchant of Prato*, 1957, pp. 271–3.

26. Montepulciano, Archivio, *Liber Apodixarum et Exitus Comunis* (*Apodisse dei Priori 8*), f. 424v. The sum demanded was 4 florins, which no doubt equalled the 16 lire 6 solidi he and the other twenty-four townsmen actually paid.

27. For these places and others in the district of Montepulciano see I. Calabresi, in Benci, *ed. cit.*, pp. 286–7.

28. For *mezzadria* and *affitto* and the economy of land-ownership in Tuscany see P. J. Jones, 'Florentine families and Florentine diaries in the fourteenth century', in *Papers of the British School at Rome*, xxiv, 1956, pp. 194–202; I. Origo, *The Merchant of Prato*, passim.

29. According to a list compiled c. 1632 by Giuliano di Simone Bagnesi (*Tavola e Nomi di Podestà, Capit., e Commissarii di Montepulciano. . . . fino al 1632*, Ms. Magl. II III 435 in Biblioteca Nazionale, Florence) Aldobrandino di Giorgio Aldobrandini was Podestà of Montepulciano from September 1428 to March 1428/9.) Archivio di Stato, Florence, *Catasto 257* (*Campioni, Distretto Montepulciano e Vagliana*), ff. 136–9. 2000 florins are noted in this as placed *'sul fondacho di filippo di bernaba degli agli'*.

30. L. Martines, *The Social World of the Florentine Humanists 1390–1460*, London, 1963, pp. 69–70, 82–3.

31. See E. Fiumi, 'Stato di popolazione e distribuzione della ricchezza in Prato secondo il catasto del 1428–9' in *Archivio storico italiano*, cxxiii, 1965, pp. 277–303.

32. 'Oratio in nebulonem maledicum' quoted in *Epistolae*, ed. Mehus, i, Florence, 1741, p. xxv.

33. A. Parigi, *Notizie del Cardinale Roberto Nobili, degli altri illustri poliziani, e della città di Montepulciano*, 1836, pp. 158–62. Messer Jacopo must have become Arciprete of Santa Maria at some date between 1389 and 1400, for in 1389 a Messer Guido Guidiccioli was Arciprete (Benci, *ed. cit.*, note on p. 153). The Arcipreti of Montepulciano had long been contumacious towards Arezzo: cf. D. Moreni, *Spoglio di pergamene del sec. xiii–xvii dell Archivio Diplomatico di Firenze* (MS Moreniano 212, in Biblioteca Riccardiana, Florence, p. 81) citing a document dated 4 October 1313 concerning a controversy between the Arciprete and Chapter of Santa Maria and the Bishop of Arezzo about rights claimed by Santa Maria and denied by the Bishop. '*Il Consulto è interessante, perchè si discute in esso la giurisdizione dei Prelati inferiori, la quale comparisce non di poco momento.*' The document is contained in the Rogati Bartolommeo di Lenzarino.

A list of the Arcipreti and Proposti of Montepulciano compiled in 1863 in the form of a painted tree of succession hangs in the sacristy of the Duomo. It gives the order of succession from 1385 as Francesco de' Piendibeni (i.e. F. da Montepulciano), 1400 Giacomo Aragazzi, 1414 Angiolo Cini, 1428 Bartolommeo Aragazzi, 1430 Corrado Bellarmino, 1458 Fabiano Benci, 1481 Pagannuccio Paganucci, 1510 Federico Paganucci, 1512 Dionigi Aragazzi, 1518 Vincenzo Aragazzi, 1543 Giovanni Ricci, 1544, Pier Francesco Nobili, 1556 Girolamo Andreucci, 1556 Spinello Benci (in 1562 first Bishop). But this list is utterly untrustworthy as to dates and names for the period 1385–1458.

34. For this see Sibilla Symeonides, *Taddeo di Bartolo* (Accademia Senese degli Intronati, Monografie d'Arte Senese, VII) Siena, 1965, pp. 88–97, 210. The inscription reads: '*Taddeo di Bartolo da Siena dipinse questa op*(er)*a al tempo di Messere Iacopo di Bartolommeo archiprete di Montepulciano Ano Dni MCCCCI.*'

35. Archivio di Stato, Florence, 96/IV, f. 60v, 16 September 1431. '*Electio nunptii pro plebe s marie . . . Constitutio canonicorum. Eodem die loco et coram testibus suprascriptis. Vniversis pateat manifeste quod convocato congregato . . . capitulo. . . . Et habito in simul colloquio et raciocinio* *de provisione fienda de vno archipresbitero cum dominus Jacobus bartolomej recolende memorie olim archipresbiter dicte plebis finem vmane nature persolverit. Et de mansione fienda per archipresbiterum in dicta ecclesia plebis sancte marie cum dictus olim dominus Jacobus nunquam steterit nec habitaverit in dicta ecclesia plebis sancte marie. Ex quo multa et innumerabilia dampna dicta ecclesia et plebs et capitulum receperunt. . . .'* To prevent this from happening again they intend to insist on the obligation of residence. Document kindly communicated by Dr. I. Calabresi.

36. Montepulciano, Archivio, *Deliberazione 29*, f. 92r.

37. *Epistolario di Guarino Veronese*, ed. R. Sabbadini, iii, 1919, p. 46, citing letter of John XXIII dated *III kal. maii anno primo* signed *B. de Montepoliciano de curia*. There are general accounts of Bartolommeo Aragazzi in G. Voigt, *Die Wiederbelebung des klassischen Alterthums*, ii, 1893, pp. 25–7; A. Castellini, in *Rivista letteraria* (pub. Udine), viii, 1936 (not seen); unsigned entry (using Castellini) in *Dizionario biografico degli italiani*, iii, 1961, pp. 686–8; A. C. de la Mare, 'Bartolommeo Aragazzi of Montepulciano', in her *The Handwriting of the Italian Humanists*, i, Oxford, 1973, pp. 85–90. I have taken Dr. de la Mare as my authority in my account of manuscripts written by Aragazzi.

38. For the organisation of the Papal Chancery see G. Mollat, *Les Papes d'Avignon*, latest ed.; B. Guillemain, *La Cour Pontificale d'Avignon 1309–76*, Paris, 1966, pp. 304–30.

39. From his funeral oration on Leonardo Bruni, printed by Mehus, in Bruni, *Epistolae, ed. cit.*, i, p. cxx.

40. Much about Francesco and a good but incomplete summary of his career in F. Novati, ed. *Epistolario di Coluccio Sabutati*, iii, 1896, pp. 312, 314, iv, 1905, pp. 3–7, 9, 17, 111; and G. Billanovich, 'Giovanni del Virgilio, Pietro da Moglio, Francesco da Fiano' in *Italia medioevale e umanistica*, vi, 1963, pp. 211–14, especially bibliography on p. 212, n. 2. To these should be added Eubel, *Hierarchia*, i, p. 104, ii, p. 105; J. Barali, *Vite de' Vescovi Aretini*, Arezzo, 1638, pp. 95–7; Marini, *Degli Archiatri Pontefcj*, ii, 1784, pp. 58–9, n. 3; Parigi, *op. cit.*, pp. 84–5;

A. Gherardi, *Statuti della Università e Studio fiorentino*, Florence, 1881, pp. 380–1 (for two letters from the Signoria of Florence to the Pope invoking Francesco as intermediary); W. von Hofmann, *Forschungen zur Geschichte der kurialen Behörden von Schisma bis zu Reformation*, 1914, i, p. 77, ii, pp. 106, 255; Finke, passim. It should be noted that Francesco has often been confused with Bartolommeo and given the name of Aragazzi.

41. See a fragment of a poem by Francesco which was printed in Mehus's introduction to his edition of Traversari's letters, i, p. 367. This is said to have been the first poem he wrote and is addressed to his teacher Ser Niccolò Niccoli of Perugia, who lectured in the metrical art at the University there from December 1389. The poem dates from 1390. For a poem addressed to Francesco by the Florentine notary Ser Domenico di Silvestro, also a friend of Salutati, see Mehus, *op. cit.*, p. 329.

42. *Epistolae, ed. cit.*, i, lib. iv, epist. v, pp. 112–13.

43. Printed in Traversari, *Epistolae, ed. cit.*, Lib. xxiv, Epist. 9 (cols. 981–5).

44. *op. cit.*, n. 23, col. 985.

45. *op. cit.*, col. 982; G. Cammelli, *I dotti bizantini e le origini dell' umanesimo. I: Manuele Crisolara*, Florence, 1941, pp. 147–8.

46. Bruni, *Epistolae*, ii, lib. vi, epist. 6, p. 50.

47. Now MS. Laur. 90, sup. 42.

48. B. L. Ullman, *The Humanism of Coluccio Salutati*, Padua, 1963, pp. 30–1. The colophon reads: '*B. de Montepoliciano ante Decembrium scribens finij Deo gratias Con(stantiae) XVI decembris MCCCCXIIII.*'

49. For this see Finke, *Acta Concilii Constanciensis*, ii, 1923, p. 234.

50. Finke, iii, pp. 542–4.

51. Letter to Traversari *cit.*

52. Guarino, *Epistolario*, ed. R. Sabbadini, i, Venice, 1915, pp. 81–3, 101–5.

53. In same MS. as the Salutati (see n. 47). The colophon reads: *Epithoma finit Augustini et Orosii eius discipuli. Finiui die VIII februarii MCCCC°XVI° Constantie B. de Montepoliciano.* The date would of course have to be interpreted as 1417 if Aragazzi was using the Florentine style. In the fifteenth century Prosper's chronicle was attributed to Augustine and Orosius. Mehus in Traversari, *Epistolae*, i, p. 381.

54. The Asconius is MS. Laur. 54,5 in the Laurenziana: the Silius Italicus is Vat. Ottob. lat. 1258. Bruni, *Epistolae*, lib. iv, epist. v. A. C. Clark, *The Vetus Cluniacensis of Poggio*, Oxford, 1905, pp. vi–vii.

55. Traversari, *Epistolae*, lib. xxiv, epist. ix.

56. F. Barbarus, *F. Barbari et aliorum ad ipsum epistolae*, ed. Quirini, Brescia, 1743, pp. 1–8; Guarino, *Epistolae, ed. cit.*, i, pp. 151–2.

57. For all these journeys in search of MSS. see R. Sabbadini, *Le scoperte dei codici latini e greci ne' secoli XIV e XV*, Florence, 1905, and A. C. de la Mare, *The Handwriting of the Italian Humanists*, i, Oxford, 1973, pp. 64–6, 85–90.

58. For some time it was the only archetype of the text. It was bought after Bartolommeo's death by the father of Antonio Barbadori, during his term of office as Podestà of Montepulciano. See Filelfo, *Epistolarium familiarium*, Venice, 1502, f. 116v, 163v, 165v: Mehus in Traversari, *op. cit.*, i, p. xxxvi; R. Sabbadini, ii, p. 282, p. 252 n.

59. MS. Pl. 51. M in the Laurenziana. The MS., which dates from the fourteenth century, was acquired by Aragazzi, who scraped out the name of the previous owner on f. 96v and inserted *B. de Montep(o)lician.* See C. Leonardi, 'I codici di Marziano Capella', in *Aevum*, xxxiii, 1959, pp. 479–80, xxxiv, 1960, pp. 40–1, No. 53.

60. Vatican Greco 2175. See G. Mercati, 'Il Plutarco di Bartolommeo da Montepulciano', in *Opere minori*, iv, Vatican City, 1937, pp. 200–4 (from *Byzantion*, i, 1924, pp. 469–74). The inscriptions on the last complete leaf are: '*Questo libro ene di iachopo danichino et chompā danchonā.*

Comperato per me piero dangiolo in chostanti-nopoli', '*De danari di Messere Bartolommeo di Francesscho di Bartolommeo da montepulciano*', '*Liber iste est mei Bartholomei de Montepol. B. de Montepolitian*'.

61. Guarino, *Epistolario*, i, p. 162, iii, p. 67.

62. L. Smith, *Epistolario di Pier Paolo Vergerio*, Rome, 1934, p. 377n.

63. Benci, *Storia di Montepulciano, ed. cit.*, p. 74.

64. See n. 72.

65. P. M. Baumgarten, *Aus Kanzlei und Kammer*, Freiburg, 1907, p. 136.

66. E. von Ottenthal, *Regulae Cancellariae Apostolicae: Die Päpstlichen Kanzelregeln von Johannes XXII bis Nicolaus V*, Innsbruck, 1888, p. 229, nos. 162, 165 (both anno VIII).

67. For a study of secretaries and secretariats see A. Kraus, 'Secretarius und Sekretariat' in *Römische Quartalschrift*, lv, 1960, pp. 43–84 (for Papal secretaries especially pp. 63–70); B. Guillemain, *La cour pontificale d'Avignon, 1309–76*, Paris, 1966, pp. 294–301.

68. Bruni, *Epistolae*, ii, lib. v, epist. 5, pp. 25–9.

69. *Commissioni*, i, p. 488, ii, pp. 227, 365.

70. For a list of Papal briefs written by Bartolommeo for Martin see K. A. Fink, 'Untersuchungen über die päpstlichen Breven des 15. Jarhunderts' in *Römische Quartalschrift*, xliii, 1935, pp. 63–4. The earliest brief listed by Fink is dated 23 March 1422.

71. B. Katterbach, *Referendarii utriusque Signaturae a Martino V ad Clementem X*, Vatican City, 1931, pp. 11–12, No. 54. Katterbach says that Bartolommeo was a secretary from 1421. He also claims that he was a protonotary, but in this he has certainly confused Bartolommeo with Francesco da Montepulciano, who did hold that high office.

72. Pius II, *De Viris aetate sua claris Aeneae Silvii opusculum*, in *Appendix ad Orationes Pii II. Pont. Max. Opuscula Quaedam Aeneae Silvii: Operis Pars III*, Lucca, 1759, ed. Mansi, p. 171, cap. xvii, listing humanists who attained distinction: '*Tam & Bartholomaeus de Montepolitiano quem Martinus Papa in secretarium recepit, atque adeo dilexit, ut unicum eum Referendarium habuerit; illique soli omnia crederet.*'

73. *Poggii Epistolae*, ed. T. Tonelli, i, Florence, 1832, lib. iii, epist. 39, pp. 287–90.

74. *op. cit.*, p. 208; B. L. Ullman, *The origin and development of humanistic script*, Rome, 1960, pp. 64–5.

75. *Poggii Epistolae*, lib. ii, epist. 8, pp. 100–3.

76. *op. cit.*

77. I have used the edition in *Poggii Florentini oratoris et philosophi opera*, Basle, 1538.

78. *Poggii Epistolae*, ed. cit., pp. 277–82.

79. Florence, *Ricc. 1133*, f. 46 (printed by Ravagli, in *Erudizione e Belle Arti*, 1906, pp. 111–13). Other verses in Munich, *clm. 14634*, f. 229: *Descriptio mortis formosissimae iuvenculae olim Bartolomeae de Matulianis de Bononia* (Voigt, *Wiederbelebung*, ii, 1893, p. 26); Padua, University, 201; Vat. lat. 6875, f. 100. See A. C. de la Mare, *op. cit.*, p. 86, n. 8.

80. Appendix C, doc. 4.

81. *ed. cit.*, lib. iii, epist. 27, pp. 283–5; for the plague see L. Mancini, *Vita di Lorenzo Valla*, Florence, 1891, pp. 20–1.

82. Mollat, *Les Papes d'Avignon, ed. cit.*, p. 370.

83. For these and all further references to the wills of Bartolommeo and Francesco see Francesco's *catasto* return, printed in Appendix C, doc. 3.

84. See Iris Origo, *The World of San Bernardino*, ed. of 1964, pp. 67–70.

85. For this see L. Martines, *op. cit.*, pp. 104, 106, 126–7.

86. Vespasiano da Bisticci, *ed. cit.*, pp. 249–50.

87. F. Baix, *La chambre apostolique et les Libri*

Annatarum de Martin V, 1417–31, i, p. 82, no. 257; pp. 194–5, no. 522; p. 257, no. 685; p. 309, no. 835; pp. 313–14, no. 849; p. 322, no. 893; p. xxx.

88. Martines, *op. cit.*, pp. 124–7.

89. For Casini, a very important figure in his day, see the life by Vespasiano da Bisticci; Ciacconius, p. 874; L. Cardella, *Memorie storiche de' cardinali della Santa Romana Chiesa*, iii, Rome, 1793, pp. 42–3; Eubel, i, pp. 34, 395, 446, 269; Bruni, *Epistolae*, i, lib. iv, epist. 16, pp. 128–9; cf. also p. 47.

90. For Lope de Olmedo and Sant' Alessio see Dom Hélyot, *Histoire des ordres monastiques, religieux et militaires, et des congrégations séculières*, iii, Paris, 1715, cap. 60, pp. 447–54; F. M. Nerini, *De templo et coenobio Sanctorum Bonifacii et Alexio historica monumenta*, Rome, 1752, pp. 73, 293, 297–303 (with engraving of tomb-slab); P. Luigi Zambarelli C.R.S., *SS. Bonifacio e Alessio all' Aventino* (Le chiese di Roma illustrate, 9), Rome, 1924, pp. 13–14, 62, fig. 19.

91. See Vespasiano da Bisticci, *ed. cit.*, pp. 246–7.

92. Guarino, *Epistolario*, iii, p. 48.

93. Baix, *op. cit.*, p. 108, n. 329. For Messer Angelo da Montepulciano, later himself a Papal secretary, see Traversari, *Epistolae*, cols. 102, 514–15, 574, 664 (letter of 17 Kal martii (13 February?) 1432, describing him as a '*iuvenis summae modestiae, & humanitatis*'), 1060–6; and Traversari's *Hodoeporicon*.

94. See p. 224.

95. He returned his age as 46 in his *catasto* return of 29 February 1429 (Archivio di Stato, Florence, *Catasto* 257, f. 245; *Catasto* 219, ff. 513–14).

96. Montepulciano, Archivio, *Liber Apodixarum et Exitus Communis* (*Apodisse dei Priori* 8), f. 461v, 31 March 1419: '*Ser Johannis bartolomei per scriptum sindicatus nobilis uiri Pieri benevenuti olim potestatis et Ser Siluestri Lodouicj de Vulterris olim notarij camparie dicti comunis 2 lire 18 soldi*'; *Liber Reformationum, 1427–9*, f. 211, 6

December 1427: '*Ser Johannes bartholomej unus ex numero consiliarorum*'; f. 30r, 25 January 1428, '*in deputatores introitus dicti comunis*'; f. 32r, 6 February 1428, f. 41v, 20 March 1428, '*officialis catasti*'; *Liber Reformationum 1433–7*, f. 41r, 21 December 1433, '*noviter extractus*'. For his journeys to Florence as *oratore* see *ib.*, f. 61v, 12 February 1434, f. 155r, 15 November 1434, f. 238, 20 August 1435, f. 401v–402r, 17 May 1437, ff. 422v–423r, 26 September 1437; *Deliberazioni 31*, f. 147, 13 March 1439.

97. Montepulciano, Archivio, *Liber Reformationum 1433–7*, f. 273, 20 November 1435, '*dominus etc.*'; *Deliberazioni 31*, 10 September 1438, '*Electio operariorum nove ecclesie snti Augustini*'.

98. Dr. I. Calabresi, in Benci, *ed. cit.*, p. 284.

99. The confusion about the site of this priory in Repetti (*Dizionario*, iv, 1841, p. 155, s.v. S. Pietro in Petrojo) is rectified by Dr. I. Calabresi (in Benci, *ed. cit.*, pp. 447, 464). For Fabiano Benci's gift of it see Parigi, *Notizie del Cardinale Roberto Nobili*, 1836, p. 89. See also Benci, *ed. cit.*, p. 157; Fulgenzio Nardi, *Abbatiae, et Monasteria . . . per Monachos & Moniales Nostrae Congregationis vel fundata. . . .* Florence, 1726, p. 9.

100. See the tree given by F. F. Benci in Appendix C, doc. 2.

101. See annotation in Benci, *ed. cit.*, p. 153.

NOTES TO CHAPTER VIII

1. See p. 221 for a fuller discussion of its date.

2. Montepulciano, Archivio, *Liber Reformationum*, f. 433–7, f. 29v.

3. Fabriczy, pp. 46, 75–6. For this enterprise see Ammirato, *Storia fiorentina*, and above all the account of it given in his *Commentari* (ed. Muratori, *R.I.S.*, Milan, 1731, cols. 1169–70) by one of the major figures of the time, Neri di Gino

Capponi. See also Moreni's notes to his edition of Baldinucci, *Vita di Filippo di Ser Brunellesco*, Florence, 1812, pp. 265–6.

4. Fabriczy, p. 76. Letters from Giuliano to Averardo describing his sojourn in North Italy are in the Archivio di Stato, Florence, *Mediceo avanti il Principato*, filza 2, 366, 23 September, from Venice; 367, 12 October, from Padua; 378, 7 November, from Padua; 381, 17 November, from Padua; 383, 24 November, from Padua; 389, 6 December, from Padua; 15 December, from Venice; 394, 16 December, from Venice; 399, 27 December, from Venice. They contain no reference to Michelozzo. Cosimo was in Verona before 18 October 1430 (see A. Fabroni, *Magni Cosmi Medicei Vita*, ii, 1788, pp. 31–3).

5. The *catasto* return made by Michelozzo's brothers is misleadingly dated 1430 by both Fabriczy and Mather. As already pointed out it is their failure to reckon by the Florentine style of dating which is responsible for the error. The return was filed in January 1431. Fabriczy (p. 64) transcribes the original of the phrase quoted as '*alchuna persona da montepulciano*', Caplow (p. 651) as '*in* Montepulciano'.

6. '. . . advertentes qualiter Michelozius Bartolomei, qui per eos fuerat electus ad intagliandum ferros quibus monetantur Monete in dicta Zecca non servivit in dicto Ministerio, sed continue fuit absens pro suis propriis negociis. . . .' These crucial documents, whose significance for Michelozzo's visit to Rome has been entirely overlooked, are printed by Orsini, *op. cit.*, pp. 187–8. They confirm Martinelli's reading of the document of 1 April 1433 printed by Guasti (*Il pergamo di Donatello pel Duomo di Prato*, Florence, 1887, p. 23) which refers to the absence in Rome of '*Donatelo e el chompagno*' (Martinelli, in *Commentari*, viii, 1957, pp. 171–3). For the *portata* of 1457 recording the debt of the Comune for work in the *cassero* of Montepulciano Fabriczy (p. 67) should be consulted, not Mather, who omits the date of 1432.

7. For the documents supporting these dates see the references to Chapter XI.

8. Michelozzo's *catasto* return of 1457 printed by Fabriczy, pp. 67–8. For Niccoli's letter see A. C. de la Mare, *The Handwriting of the Italian*

Humanists, Oxford, 1973, pp. 59–61, pl. xiiia. Leonardo di Giorgio can perhaps be identified as Leonardo di Giorgio del Biada (see p. 175).

9. Vasari, ii, ed. Milanesi, p. 434.

10. Orsini, *op. cit.*, pp. 189–91.

11. For Prato see the references on pp. 284–5. The documents concerning Messer Jacopo are all in the Archivio di Stato, Florence and are printed in Appendix C, docs. 5 & 6. They were kindly communicated by Dr. I. Calabresi.

12. Printed by H. Saalman, 'The Palazzo Comunale in Montepulciano', in *Zeitschrift für Kunstgeschichte*, xxviii, 1965, pp. 36–7. For the *catasto* of 1469 see Fabriczy, pp. 68–9.

13. Montepulciano, Archivio, *Liber Reformationum*, ff. 249r, 250r. Printed as Appendix C, doc. 7.

14. Montepulciano, Archivio, *Copialettera 2* (no foliation) and *Liber Reformationum 1433–7*, ff. 328, 331r. Printed as Appendix C, docs. 8, 9 & 10. For the annulment of 21 May 1436 see Archivio di Stato, Florence, Archivio Diplomatico, Spoglio 2, Parte 6, Comune di Montepulciano, c. 256, *cit.* Caplow, *Michelozzo*, i, 1977, p. 239.

15. Montepulciano, Archivio, *Liber Reformationum, 1433–7*, ff. 400v, 401v–402r; *Copialettera 3*, f. 10r. Printed in Appendix C, docs. 11, 12 & 13.

16. Montepulciano, Archivio, *Copialettera 3*, f. 17v. Printed as Appendix C, doc. 14.

17. Printed by Fabriczy, pp. 78–80.

18. Documents printed by Saalman, *op. cit.*, pp. 36–7.

19. See Appendix C, doc. 19.

20. Montepulciano, Archivio, *Copialettera 3*, no foliation. Printed in Appendix C, doc. 15.

21. Archivio, Montepulciano, *Liber Reformationum 1437–41*, f. 199r. Printed as Appendix C, doc. 16.

22. Montepulciano, Archivio, *Liber Reformationum 1437–41*, ff. 200r, 200v. Printed in Appendix C, doc. 17.

23. Montepulciano, Archivio, *Copialettera 3*, f. 66v. Printed as Appendix C, doc. 18.

24. *S. Instrumentum Processus super Statu Ecclesiae Politianensis*, 3 January 1597. MS. in the Archivio of the Duomo of Montepulciano.

25. S. Benci, *Storia di Montepulciano, ed. cit.*, pp. 80–1.

26. The attribution made on the basis of a document of 1460, published by Saalman (*op. cit.*) is queried by Dr. Calabresi (in Benci, *ed. cit.*, pp. 466–7, s.v. campanile) who prints other documents showing that the campanile was rebuilt in 1476. The question, he tells me in a letter, has recently been complicated by the discovery on 23 May 1971 that one of the four bells of the campanile is dated 1462.

27. *Instrumentum, cit.* f. 9 ff. Don Luca Filicelli, 'la Chiesa vecchia . . . che ha tre Naui con le sue colonnate', f. 17v, Canonico Dominico Danese, 'la Chiesa è antica . . . ha il suo Coro con le sue sedie di legno di noce distinte secondo li gradi . . . la mensa episcopale ha l'habitatione ma angusta, et piccola, ma quelle poche stanze, che ui sono, son buone, la quale sta attacata alla Chiesa, nella quale ui sono quattro Camere buone et una Sala'; f. 22, Spinello Benci (later bishop), 'Non è molto grande, ma è capace, per quel popolo . . . non ha bisogno di riparatione alcuna'; f. 27v, Canonico Cristoforo Rughesi, 'la Chiesa non è molto bella, ne molto grande per esser struttura antica, ma ha tre navicelle, con le sue colonne'; f. 39r, Sallustio Tarugi, 'la Chiesa è antica piccola con due ordini di colonne et tre naui, et perché non è capace per il popolo se ne fabrica una più maggiore et più insigne'.

28. Parigi, *Notizie del Cardinale Roberto Nobili, degli altri illustri poliziani, e della città di Montepulciano*, Montepulciano, 1836, pp. 87–8, no. 71.

29. See Mancusi-Ungaro, *Michelangelo: the Bruges Madonna and the Piccolomini Altar*, 1971, passim.

NOTES TO CHAPTER IX

1. Vasari, ed. Milanesi, ii, 1878, pp. 413–14. For the rebuilding see R. Bonelli, 'Ippolito Scalza e il Duomo di Montepulciano', in *Bullettino Senese di Storia Patria*, n.s. x(xvii), 1939, pp. 1–10: [Don Idro Marcocci], *Per conoscere Montepulciano*, 1965, pp. 63–6.

2. Parigi, *Notizie*, 1836, pp. 92–4, 88–97, 162–3.

3. Dempster, *op. cit.*, ii, Florence, 1724, p. 425. Benci, *ed. cit.*, p. 74. Benci's book was first published in 1641; the passage is the same in both editions. For Benci see *Dizionario biografico degli italiani*, viii, Rome, 1966, pp. 200–1.

4. (G. Bartoli), *Istoria di S. Agnese di Montepulciano con delle memorie della medesima città, e suoi uomini illustri*, Siena, 1779, pp. 124–5.

5. E. Fumi, *Guida di Montepulciano e dei Bagni di Chianciano*, 1894, pp. 54–5.

6. It has an inscription of the same date.

7. E. Repetti, *Dizionario*, iii, Florence, 1839, p. 481.

8. See J. C. Robinson (*Catalogue of the Special Exhibition . . . at the South Kensington Museum*, 1863, p. 2, nos. 15–16) and Pope-Hennessy and Lightbown, *Catalogue of Italian Sculpture in the Victoria & Albert Museum*, i, 1964, p. 100.

9. Bode, *Denkmäler der Renaissance-Skulptur Toscanas*, Munich, 1892–1905, pp. 47–8, Taf. 168.

10. For the secondary literature of the Aragazzi tomb and of the Sant' Agostino figures (pp. 228–9) see, besides the works already cited or to be cited, M. Reymond, *La sculpture florentine: première moitié du XVe siècle*, Florence, 1898, pp. 161–4; Wolff, 1900, pp. 40–59; Venturi, *Storia*, vi, 1908, pp. 349–64 and viii, pt. I, 1923, pp. 269–70; Pope-Hennessy and Lightbown, *Catalogue of Italian Sculpture in the Victoria & Albert Museum*, i, London, 1964, pp. 100–3.

11. '. . . *nullus prelatus de cetero audeat ad Pala-*

tium venire nisi in capa, et sic quando vadunt per Curiam. Et idem dicitur de Auditoribus.' Printed by C. Guasti, '*Gli avanzi dell' archivio di un pratese vescovo di Volterra*', in *Archivio storico italiano*, ser. 4, xiii, 1884, pp. 340–1, where the proper habit of Papal *cubicularii* is also given as '*cum guarnacia et caputeo*', and that of *scriptores litterarum apostolicarum* as '*tabardo cum caputeo*'.

12. Longhurst, C.12.

13. See note 11. Burckhardt, *Liber Notarum*, i, pp. 24–5, 26 August 1484, '*In hac missa et in aliis novem exequialibus . . . celebratis, prelati curie interfuerunt sine cappis, sed in eorum mantellis cum suis cappucciis circa collum transversatis more solito.*' For the *tabarro* see R. Levi Pisetzky, *Storia del Costume in Italia*, ii, Milan, 1964, pp. 54–5.

14. See E. Polidori-Calamandrei, *Le vesti delle donne fiorentine nel quattrocento*, Florence, 1924, pp. 35 ff., 52, 88.

15. The sexes of these youths were muddled by Schmarsow ('Nuovi studi', in *Arch. St. dell' Arte*, vi, 1893, pp. 243–4) who mistakenly identified two of them as girls. Is there any need to point out that semi-naked girls would never have been represented on a relief of this kind, intended for a tomb? Compare the costume of the girl in the other relief.

16. The identification appears to go back to John Addington Symonds and Paul Bourget (see next chapter).

17. The analogies with Donatello were first recognised by Bode who went so far as to attribute their design to him (in Burckhardt, *Der Cicerone*, 4th ed., ii, Leipzig, 1879, p. 356). Schmarsow (*op. cit.*, pp. 245–6) rightly reacts against this view.

18. Vasari, ed. Milanesi, ii, p. 432.

19. Bode (in Burckhardt, *Der Cicerone*, ed. of 1879, *loc. cit.*) had already recognised it as a Blessing Christ. Schmarsow (*op. cit.*, p. 248) was responsible for this identification, another sample of how the positive achievements of his great stylistic acuteness were marred by his indifference to the historical and antiquarian considerations which might have assisted him to form a better total judgement.

20. G. Kaftal, *Iconography of the Saints in Tuscan painting*, Florence, 1952, pp. 138–40; *Iconography of the Saints in the Central and South Italian Schools of Painting*, Florence, 1965, cols. 154–8.

22. For the Piccolomini chapel-tomb see R. Mancusi-Ungaro, Jr., *Michelangelo, the Bruges Madonna and the Piccolomini Altar*, New Haven, London, 1971. The letter of 1511 is on p. 98. For the figure attributed to Giovanni Dalmata and thought to have formed part of the destroyed tomb of Pope Nicholas V (d. 1455) in St. Peter's, see R. U. Montini, *Le tombe dei Papi*, Rome, 1957. It is now in the Sacre Grotte Vaticane.

23. C. Seymour, Jr., 'Some aspects of Donatello's methods of figure and space construction . . .' in Istituto Nazionale di Studi sul Rinascimento, *Donatello e il suo tempo*, Florence, 1968, pp. 195–206.

NOTES TO CHAPTER X

1. Gaye, *Carteggio inedito d'artisti*, i, Florence, 1839, p. 118.

2. Perkins, *op. cit.*, i, pp. 143–5.

3. Symonds, *Italian Byways*, 1883, pp. 41–63; Bourget, *Sensations d'Italie*, cap. ix, letter of 1 November 1890.

4. Vol. x, 1887, fasc. vi, tav. iv.

5. See E. Fumi, *Guida di Montepulciano e dei Bagni di Chianciano*, Montepulciano, 1894, pp. 54–5.

6. Burger, p. 131. Recently, Harriet Caplow (*Michelozzo*, i, 1977, pp. 210–349) has produced another study of the tomb. Not having traced the contemporary documents about Aragazzi and his family and the history of his tomb on which this study is founded, she makes a number of errors in the identification of the figures. Thus, in spite of the absence of a halo, she identifies the old cleric as the Beato Bartolommeo Pucci-Franceschi (d. *c.* 1330), who became a Franciscan in his old age and was the object of a local cult in Montepulciano for centuries before his eventual beatification in 1880. She follows this up with a suggestion that the matron and children represent Camilla, the saintly wife of the Beato and their four sons. The extreme implausibility of this interpretation is obvious.

Again on the mistaken supposition that Aragazzi himself prescribed the programme for his tomb, she identifies the left-hand angel as Rhetoric, claiming for the figure a deliberate sexual ambiguity more in keeping with French *fin-de-siècle* decadence than with the robust explicitness of the *quattrocento*. The St. Michael she identifies as Cicero. These identifications rest on a misapprehension of the nature and purpose of tomb-sculpture in the *quattrocento* and on the essential function of the tomb as an incitement to prayer for the deceased. A similar misunderstanding of the doctrines of justification that underlie the iconography of tombs from the thirteenth to the fifteenth centuries leads her to interpret the figure of the Blessing Christ as the Apostle Bartholomew.

Harriet Caplow is now doubtful about her earlier reconstructions of the tomb and accordingly they are not detailed here.

7. Printed in Appendix C, doc. 19.

8. Montepulciano, Archivio Vescovile, *Visitatio Ecclesiae, et Dioc.⁸ Montis Politiani. Anno 1610*, f. 4v: '*Die Martis 20 Aprilis. De Visitatione Altarium Cathedralis Ecclesiae. . . . Altare Sᵗⁱ Angeli. Rᵐᵘˢ D. Visitator comperuit fuisse adimpletum decretum de demoliendo altare S. Angeli iuxta formam decreti visitationis apostolicae quod laudavit, et se informauit quod duo tituli beneficiorum vnus S. Angeli primi et alter S. angeli s.ᵈⁱ sunt translati ad altare S. Caterinae primus possidetur a D. lud.ᶜᵒ Aragatio. . . .' Ib.*, Libro C, Visitation of Cardinal Roberto Ubaldini, f. 20v; *ib.* Visitation of June 1641 by the Bishop of Montepulciano, f. 6v.

9. W. Rolfs, *Neapel*, ii, *Baukunst und Bildnerei*, Leipzig, 1905, pp. 145–6, 109, 112.

10. Venturi (*Storia*, iv, 1906, pp. 498–505, wrongly attributed to Nino Pisano). For its date see A. Da Mosto, *I Dogi di Venezia*, Milan, 1960, pp. 135–8.

11. For the Capranica tomb, which is attributed to Paolo Romano, see L. Ciaccio, 'L'ultimo periodo della scultura gotica a Roma', in *Ausonia*, i, 1907, pp. 84–5; Filippini, *La scultura nel trecento a Roma*, Rome, 1908, pp. 164–8; A. Muñoz, 'Meister Paolo da Gualdo', in *Monatshefte für Kunstwissenschaft*, iv, 1911, pp. 73–6. For the Geraldini tomb see G. Brunetti, 'Sul periodo "amerino" di Agostino di Duccio', in *Commentari*, xvi, 1965, pp. 47–55, with previous bibliography.

12. Pierre Ameilh, *Ordo Romanus XV*, cap. 153, in Mabillon, *Musaeum Italicum*, ii, Paris, 1724, p. 537. H. von Tschudi, *Donatello e la critica moderna*, Turin, 1887, p. 11, correctly divined that this figure was an angel.

13. Again the interpretation stems back to Schmarsow (*op. cit.*). Because of it the relief is usually entitled *Il Congedo*. But Schmarsow supposed that the matron was Aragazzi's wife, and that she is here shown taking leave of her husband, surrounded by their children!

14. In Burckhardt, *Der Cicerone*, ed. Bode, ii, Leipzig, 1879, p. 356.

15. See Iris Origo, *The Merchant of Prato*, London, 1957, pp. 306–24; 'Ricordi di Cristofano Guidini' in *Archivio storico italiano*, iv, 1843, p. 40.

16. See W. R. Valentiner, 'Studies in Italian Gothic Plastic Art: 1, Tino di Camaino' in *Art in America*, xi, 1923, pp. 304–5; id., *Tino di Camaino*, Paris, 1935, pp. 115–19, 153, pl. 57). Formerly in the collection of Mr. Henry Goldman, New York, who acquired it in 1923 from Contini-Bonacossi in Rome. Identified by Valentiner as a votive relief commissioned by Queen Sancia of Naples.

17. *Breviarium Romanum*, Paris, 1528, *Commendationes animarum*, f. lxxxiiij^v.

18. *Breviarium Romanum*, Paris, 1528, *Commendationes animarum*, f. lxxxvi.

19. See Ciacconius, cols. 1027–8, 982, 1023, 1072, 1043, 993, 1088–9.

20. For the Orsi tomb, which was executed after the Bishop's death between 9 June 1320–6 February 1321 and probably before 18 July 1321, see W. Valentiner, *Tino di Camaino*, Paris, 1935, pp. 62–74. The Bishop was far from being a humble and retiring saint: an ardent Guelf, he construed his duty to the Church as justifying armed resistance by himself and his priests to the Imperial troops during a siege of Florence.

21. The inscriptions and the other essential documentary references to the tomb are printed by G. Filangieri, *Documenti per la storia le arti e le industrie delle provincie napoletane*, ii, Naples, 1884, pp. 98–101.

22. H. Baron, *Leonardo Bruni Aretino Humanistisch – Philosophische Schriften*, Leipzig, 1928, p. 210.

23. See p. 199.

24. Fabriczy, pp. 68–9. It is obvious from the documents already quoted in Chapter VIII that his statement was rigorously exact.

25. It is so called, for example, by G. Holmes, *The Florentine Enlightenment*, London, 1969, pp. 194–5.

26. See L. Berti, *Masaccio*, London, 1967, pp. 115–16, pp. 157–8, n. 270. Among painted tombs in Santa Maria Novella was one of the Beata Villana. It is possibly not without significance for the *Trinità* that Ammirato (*Istorie fiorentine*, I, pt. 2, Florence, 1647, p. 1021) calls Lorenzo Lenzi an '*uomo nuovo*'. J. Coolidge, 'Further observations on Masaccio's *Trinity*' in *Art Bulletin*, xlviii, 1966, p. 382 ff., comes within a hair's breadth of the correct solution: had he been aware of the custom of referring to an altar cum tomb as a *cappella* he would have reached it in his brilliant little article.

27. Valla, *op. cit.*, ed. of Cologne, 1527, pp. 200–1: '. . . *apud Martinum me accusasti . . . una cum Antonio Lusco collega tuo, cui me accusaveras, me ausum reprehendere scripta illius Antonij, ob id videlicet, quod apud Cyprianum Pistoriensem ad sepulturam Bartholomei Montepoliciani dixissem* *carmen in illius monumento inscriptum ab Antonio compositum versu elegiaco non esse tam egregium, quàm alia quae hexametris versibus condidisset, melioremque poetam in eo carminis genere Bartholomeum extitisse, & penè omnium optimum. Quod dixi, quia & ita sentiebam, & me ille ad studia solitus fuerat hortari'* (passage first noted by Cardinal Quirini, *Diatriba praeliminaris in duas partes divisa ad Francisci Barbari . . . epistolas*, Brescia, 1741, p. 6). See also L. Mancini, *Vita di Lorenzo Valla*, Florence, 1891, pp. 20-1.

28. Pastor, *ed. cit.*, i, p. 43n.

29. Cf. Francesco's *catasto* return. Almost certainly the slab covered his *deposito* or temporary resting-place after interment.

30. Schmarsow, *op. cit.*, pp. 252-55.

31. He could have done so from Benci, cf. p. 182.

32. Bode, *Florentiner Bildhauer der Renaissance*, 1902, p. 59.

33. Morisani, p. 89 (citing other secondary literature); Saalman, *op. cit.*, p. 51.

34. Fumi, *op. cit.*, p. 28, who records a tradition that the façade was designed by Arnolfo di Lapo.

35. Information kindly communicated by Dr. I. Calabresi, who also tells me that there is a mention of work on the new church in 1408. See also Repetti (*ed. cit.*, pp. 181-2).

36. Montepulciano, Archivio, *Deliberazioni 29*, f. 92r.

37. Montepulciano, Archivio, *Deliberazioni 31*, f. 85r; 'Electio operariorum nove ecclesie santi Augustinj.'

38. For this see H. Saalman's exemplary article, 'The Palazzo Comunale in Montepulciano: an unknown work by Michelozzo', in *Zeitschrift für Kunstgeschichte*, xxviii, 1965, pp. 1-46.

39. The date is imperfectly legible from ground level but must be either 1507 or 1508 (an opinion in which Dr. I. Calabresi concurs).

Schmarsow (*op. cit.*, p. 254) who also reads it as 1508, states that the *Memorie* of the church recorded that '*la facciata dal secondo cornicione in su fu compita nel 1509*'.

40. This seems to be the correct interpretation, since *fraternitas* governs *clericorum*. But there was a Fraternità di Sant' Agostino which is mentioned in 1630 (Archivio Vescovile, Duomo, Montepulciano, *Miscellanea Sanctae Politianae Ecclesiae Liber Secundus* (B²), ff. 28, 67, '*La Fraternità di Sant' Agostino. Vnita con l'Opera. Questa fraternita suol esser governata dai principali Cittadini sepultuarij di quella Chiesa*'). A lay confraternity, it is known to have formed one body with the *Opera* at least as early as 1552.

41. Schmarsow, *op. cit.*, p. 250n.

42. Vasari, ed. Milanesi, ii, p. 462. For Pasquino see Fabriczy, in *Rivista d'Arte*, iv, 1906, p. 27; R. Nuti, 'Pasquino di Matteo da Montepulciano e le sue sculture nel Duomo di Prato', in *Bulletino senese di storia patria*, x, 1939, pp. 338 ff.; G. Marchini, 'Di Maso di Bartolommeo e d'altri', in *Commentari*, iii, 1952, pp. 108-27.

NOTES TO CHAPTER XI

1. G. M. Bianchini, *Notizie istoriche intorno alla Sacratissima Cintola di Maria Vergine*, Florence, 1722 (attestation of the Accademia Fiorentina dated 6 August 1721), pp. 1-4.

2. *op. cit.*, pp. 33-7.

3. Sant' Antonino, *Summa historica*, pt. 1, tit. 6, cap. 10, $1.

4. C. Guasti, *Il pergamo di Donatello pel Duomo di Prato*, Florence, 1887, p. 10.

5. Bianchini, *op. cit.*, pp. 59-60.

6. Guasti, *op. cit.*, pp. 10-11. Cf. also the note by G. Marchini, *Il Duomo di Prato*, Milan, 1957, p. 57, about the site of one of the early pulpits.

7. Bianchini, *op. cit.*, pp. 65-7.

8. Guasti, p. 11. Four reliefs representing the Death of the Virgin, her Assumption and gift of her Girdle to St. Thomas, her Coronation and Thomas's gift of the girdle have been identified, almost certainly correctly, as the remains of this pulpit (see Marchini, *Duomo di Prato*, pp. 56-7). Given the unfinished condition of the Coronation, Marchini doubts whether it was ever mounted on the pulpit.

9. Marchini, *Il pulpito donatelliano del Duomo di Prato*, Prato, 1966, pp. 5-6.

10. Guasti, *op. cit.*, p. 12.

11. Printed by Guasti, *op. cit.* pp. 12-15. It followed a resolution made by the *Difensori* and *Gonfaloniere* of Prato two days before, on 12 July.

12. See H. Glasser, 'The litigation concerning Luca della Robbia's Federighi tomb' in *Mitteilungen des Kunsthistorischen Instituts in Florenz*, xiv, 1969-70, pp. 24-32.

13. Guasti, p. 23.

14. Printed by Guasti, pp. 15-16.

15. M. Lisner, 'Zur frühen Bildhauerarchitektur Donatellos', in *Münchner Jahrbuch der bildenden Kunst*, ser. 3, ix-x, 1958-9, pp. 117-18, docs. 3-6; Guasti, pp. 26-7.

16. Lisner, pp. 118-19, docs. 14-26.

17. Lisner, p. 119, doc. 28.

18. Guasti, p. 23, doc. 2; Lisner, p. 119, doc. 30.

19. Guasti, p. 23, doc. 2.

20. Lisner, p. 119, doc. 31.

21. Lisner, pp. 118-19, docs. 11, 18, 20, 21, 25.

22. Janson, p. 113.

23. Lisner, doc. 11.

24. Lisner, p. 123, doc. 88.

25. Lisner, pp. 85-90.

26. Lisner, p. 120, doc. 34.

27. For the documentation of the Cantoria see Janson, pp. 119-22. I retain the term *cantoria* for convenience.

28. Lisner, p. 120, docs. 38, 47; p. 121, doc. 52; p. 120, doc. 48 (2 September); p. 121, doc. 54 (16 October), doc. 56 (3 November), doc. 57 (9 November), doc. 58 (11 November), doc. 59 (20 November), doc. 60 (17 December); doc. 61 (18 December); Guasti, p. 20 (9 December).

29. See Guasti, pp. 20-1; Lisner, p. 122, docs. 74, 76 and the acute analysis of Janson (pp. 114-15) made before the publication of Dr. Lisner's documents.

30. Lisner, p. 120, docs. 39, 40, 44, 46; docs. 42, 43.

31. Printed by Guasti, pp. 17-19.

32. Printed by Guasti, p. 19.

33. Lisner, p. 121, docs. 64, 68; Guasti, p. 24, doc. 5.

34. Lisner, p. 122, doc. 84; Guasti, p. 25, docs. 12, 13, 14.

35. For Maso in general see G. Marchini, 'Di Maso di Bartolommeo e d'altri' in *Commentari*, iii, 1952, pp. 108-27.

36. Lisner, pp. 121-2, docs. 65, 66, 70, 71, 72; Guasti, p. 25, doc. 10.

37. Guasti, p. 24, doc. 9.

38. Lisner, p. 122, docs. 74, 76.

39. Lisner, p. 122, docs. 79, 82, 83.

40. Lisner, p. 123, docs. 87, 88, 89-93.

41. Lisner, p. 123, docs. 94, 95, 96.

42. Lisner, pp. 123-4, docs. 97, 98. Marchini (*op. cit.*, pp. 16-17) points out that the agreement of 1436 must refer only to the three panels which Donatello sent for that year, that one of them was left unfinished, and that on the adjudication

of the *Signoria* this was completed and the three other reliefs hastily executed.

43. Lisner, p. 124, doc. 100.

44. Guasti, p. 25, doc. 15; Marchini, *op. cit.*, p. 17.

45. Guasti, p. 26, doc. 17.

46. G. Marchini, *Il pulpito donatelliano*, 1966, p. (25) facing figs. 13–14.

47. Marchini, *op. cit.*, p. 35.

48. Lisner, p. 118, doc. 4; p. 119, doc. 26; p. 120, doc. 50; p. 121, doc. 51; p. 121, doc. 52.

49. Kauffmann, p. 72.

50. See Janson, p. 127; *id.*, 'Donatello and the antique', in Istituto Nazionale di Studi sul Rinascimento, *Donatello e il suo tempo*, Florence, 1968, pp. 81–2.

51. See preceding note.

52. See the letter of 28 September 1428 from Nanni di Miniato to Matteo Strozzi (p. 262, n. 28): significant in this connection too is a letter from Poggio to Niccoli from Rome (*Epistolae*, ed. Tonelli, lib. 14, epist. 12, pp. 322–4) in which he speaks of a journey by Francesco of Pistoia to Chios and of the statues he has found for him. *'Ego etiam hic aliquid habeo quod in patriam portabitur. Donatellus vidit, et summe laudavit.'* This letter, dated 23 September, is referred by Tonelli to 1430. If he is correct, it is of interest as recording a visit by Donatello to Rome.

53. Piero Chellini of Florence was paid 2 florins on 3 September 1438 for gilding the capital, shields and lilies of the arms of Prato (Guasti, p. 26, doc. 16). For other details of colouring see Marchini (*op. cit.*, p. 27).

54. Marchini (*loc. cit.*).

55. Guasti, pp. 27–8, docs. 19–20.

56. Printed by Marchini, *op. cit.*, p. 30.

57. Vasari, ed. Milanesi, ii, p. 444 (wrongly dated after Cosimo's death).

58. C. F. Berti, *Cenni storico-artistici per servire di guida ed illustrazione alla insigne basilica di S. Miniato al Monte*, Florence, 1850, p. 151; 'San Giovanni Gualberto' in Istituto Giovanni XXIII, *Bibliotheca Sanctorum*, vi, 1965, cols. 1012–32.

59. Compare for instance the similar restriction laid by Jacopo di Ottavio di Bongianni di Mino in 1494 on the nuns of Santa Chiara after he had rebuilt their church (Pope-Hennessy and Lightbown, *Catalogue of Italian Sculpture in the Victoria and Albert Museum*, i, London, 1964, p. 178).

60. For these two documents, taken not from the original books of the *Arte*, which are now lost, but from the *Spogli Strozziani*, see Fabriczy, p. 53.

61. See H. W. Janson, 'Two problems in Florentine Renaissance sculpture', in *Art Bulletin*, xxiv, 1942, p. 327.

62. Vasari, *Le Vite*, i, 1550, p. 353: *'Et nella Nunziata auendo contratto amicitia con COSIMO vecchio de' Medici; & auendo molto dato opera alla architettura lauorò di marmo la cappella di essa vergine. & di bronzo gettò vn luminario, che dinanzi a quella si vede; & la pila di marmo con vn San Giovanni a sommo, & la Nostra donna mezo rilieuo sopra il desco delle candele.'* In his second edition Vasari assigned all these works to Pagno, and said that the St. John Baptist was *'nel mezo'* of the stoup, and that the bench was the one at which the friars sold candles (Vasari, ii, pp. 446–7).

63. Lisner, p. 121, doc. 62 (see her note 21, p. 126).

64. A. Lensi, 'Una scultura sconosciuta di Michelozzo' in *Dedalo*, ii, 1921–2, pp. 358–62. The attribution of the relief is entirely due to Lensi, who found it while in charge of restorations in the Annunziata in a niche in a dark corridor at the top of the stair-case of the convent, and removed it to its modern position above the desk for candles in the entrance to the church under the impression that it was Michelozzo's relief. The lost St. John has, strangely, sometimes been identified with the terracotta altar statue Michelozzo made for the chapel of Antonio da Rabatta in the Annunziata (see below) and also with a bronze statuette in the Bargello. Vasari implies that it was of marble.

65. R. de Roover, *Il banco Medici*, 1970, pp. 287, 510; N. Rubinstein, *The government of Florence under the Medici (1434 to 1494)*, Oxford, 1966, p. 102n.; Tonini, *Il Santuario della Santissima Annunziata di Firenze*, Florence, 1876, pp. 118–20 (for the foundation and history of the chapel).

66. Bocchi-Cinelli, *Le Bellezze di Firenze*, Florence, 1677, pp. 439–40; Del Migliore, *Firenze città nobilissima*, 1684, pp. 282–3.

67. A. Schmarsow, *Donatello*, Breslau, 1886, p. 25; Fabriczy, pp. 55–6.

68. Lensi, *op. cit.*; Florence, *Rassegna Mensile*, i, 1932, n. 9/10, p. 88.

69. Again the original books of the *Arte* are lost, but they were examined in the eighteenth century by the Proposto Antonio Francesco Gori ('Monumenta sacrae vetustatis insignia Basilicae Baptisterii Florentini' in *Thesaurus Veterum Diptychorum*, iii, Florence, 1759, pp. 310–14).

70. The documentation of the altar, so far as it is known, is assembled by L. Becherucci, 'Il dossale d'argento', in L. Becherucci and G. Brunetti, *Il Museo dell' Opera del Duomo a Firenze*, ii, Florence, s.d., pp. 215–29 (see also pp. 5–8).

71. Gori, *loc. cit.*

72. Archivio di Stato, Florence, *Spoglio secondo delle Scritture dell' Arte di Calimala* (Carte Strozziane, ser. 2, cod. 51.2), f. 115v (111v), '*Figura d'Argento di S. Gio. bat^a che è nel Dossale d'Argento peso U.14 S.11 a Lega di d^i 11, La quale fè Michelozzo di Bartolommeo e costò f. 206, 41.5.3. Libro Grande S(egna)^{to} AA 1452, f. 177*'; f. 117, '*A Michelozzo di Bartolomeo Intagliatore si dà a fare una figura di S. Gio. bat^a d'Ariento per mettere nel Dossale dell' Ariento e per sua manifattura dee hauere f. 50.1452 Quaderno d^o* (i.e. rogato Sr Francesco Guardi, from 1450 to 1453), f. 146; f. 123v (119), '*Figura d'Argento di S. Gio bat.^{a} da mettersi nel Tabernacolo del Dossale d'Argento nella Chiesa di S. Gio. si dà à fare a*

Michelozzo del q. Bartolomeo di Gherardo da fi.^{ze} Intagliatore, la qual figura doueua essere alta un braccio e un ventesimo di braccio e doueua pesare più tosto meno che più de U.11 e per fattura doueua hauere f. 50. E questo fu l'anno 1452. Delib. dal 1451 al 1454. 12, 13, 56, 69. S'indora i peli di d^o Santo libro d.^{o} 62.'

73. To Michelozzo have also been ascribed the decorative sculptures of the palace of the Medici bank in Milan (1462–68) whose terracotta portal and medallions are now in the Castello Sforzesco, and of the Cappella di San Pietro Martire, in the church of Sant' Eustorgio, Milan (erected from *c.* 1462–68). The attribution is to be rejected (for the literature of these two works see Morisani, pp. 96–7). Also to be rejected is Ragghianti's attribution to Michelozzo of a reliquary bust now exhibited in the Museo Nazionale, Pisa (C. L. Ragghianti, 'Un busto di Michelozzo', in *Critica d'Arte*, i, 1936, pp. 139–40). Even more unacceptable is Longhi's attribution of a marble bust, of hybrid style, formerly in a Roman private collection ('Un busto di Michelozzo', in *Vita artistica*, ii, 1926, pp. 16–18). For a number of other sculptures attributed to Michelozzo see M. Reymond, *La sculpture florentine: première moitié du XVe siècle*, Florence, 1898, pp. 167–8; Venturi, *Storia*, vi, 1908, pp. 363–8. A Madonna and Child in the Musée des Beaux-Arts, Budapest, is also attributed to Michelozzo. See also Krautheimer, *Lorenzo Ghiberti*, 1970, pp. 87–8, n. 5 for a discussion and bibliography of two Annunciation figures on the niche of Ghiberti's St. Matthew on Or San Michele which have been attributed to Michelozzo. A silver crucifix figure in the treasury of San Lorenzo, Florence, is attributed to Michelozzo by A. Parronchi, 'Un crocefisso d'argento in San Lorenzo', in *Festschrift Ulrich Middeldorf*, Berlin, 1968, pp. 143–9, pl. 79–83.

A more serious problem is presented by the Madonna and Child in the Bargello. The figures are more or less related to the Virgin and Child of the Sant' Agostino lunette of *c.* 1436, with which they must be more or less contemporary if the relief is genuine. Although accepted by a long line of scholars from its first discovery by Bode (*Denkmäler*, p. 50, pl. 173a) in a Florentine private collection, this relief has a glacial quality which makes me doubt its authenticity. The Late Gothic frame and the background inlaid with blue glass are also features that excite suspicion.

Documents, Glossary,
Tables and Chronologies

Appendix A

Document 1

FLORENCE, ARCHIVIO DI STATO,
MEDICEO AVANTI IL PRINCIPATO, 89, NO. 6
BULL OF MARTIN V OF 2 JULY 1418
CONCERNING COSSA

'Martinus episcopus servus servorum dei.
Dilectis filiis Thome tituli sanctorum Johannis
et Pauli. Brande tituli sancti Clementis et Antonio
tituli sancte Cicilie presbiteris et Raynaldo sancti
viti in macello diacono sancte romane ecclesie
Cardinalibus salutem et apostolicam benedictionem. Ex certis rationabilibus causis animum
nostrum mouentibus ad hec / auctoritate apos-
tolica et ex certa scientia / Circumspectionj vestre
tenore presentium policemur. Quod Baldassari
Cosse olim Johannis xxiij in eius obedientia
nuncupato de statu quocunque honorabili ac
provisionibus pro eius statu tenendo decenter
prouidebimus illis modis gradibus condicionibus
atque formis / ac rebus et bonis tam ecclesiasticis
quam mundanis et pro illis temporibus pro ut et
quemadmodum circumspectioni vestre uisum
fuerat convenire et duxeratis declarandum /
Super quibus scientia ac auctoritate predictis
prefate circumspectioni vestre plenam et liberam
harum serie concedimus potestatem ratum et
gratum habiturj quidquid per eandem circum-
spectionem vestram factum fuerit in premissis
idque faciemus inuiolabiliter obseruarj. Nulli
ergo omnino hominum liceat hanc paginam
nostre policitationis potestatis et decreti infrin-
gere uel ei ausu temerario contrauenire. Si quis
autem hoc attemptare presumserit indignationem
omnipotentis dei et beatorum petrj et paulj
apostolorum eius se nouerit incursurum. Datum
Gebennis vj. nonas Julij pontificatus nostri anno
primo.

De Curia

F. de Montepoliciano   Registrata in
                              Camera apostolica,

Endorsed: 'Copia della bolla del Ghaleotto aura
fatto?'

'Quarto et ultimo prouisionem iterum deliberatam et factam super infrascriptis omnibus et
singulis per dictos dominos Priores vexilliferum
gonfalonieris societatis populi et duodecim bonos
viros dicti Comunis florentie secundum ordinamenta dicti Comunis que talis est videlicet
Dilectionem et antiquam beniuolentiam continuis beneficijs demonstratam per reuerendis-
simum in Christo patrem et dominum dominum
Baldassare Coscia sancte romane ecclesie cardinalem sua affectione il cardinale di firenze
uulgariter nuncupatum erga Magnificum et
potentem Comunem florentie tam tempore feli-
citatis dum papatui praefuit quam alio et ante et
post cunctos diligens florentinos et eorum statum
ut se et suum / conceptum sue mentis clarius
atque feruentius In uite exitu euidentissime pro-
bationibus Demonstrando ut erat toto populo
florentino caram et acceptam obstendere
cupientes Magnifici et potentes domini domini
priores artium et uexillifer Justitie populi et
comunis florentini. Et praecipue in sui corporis
sepultura Ideo habite super his Inuicem et una
cum officialibus gonfalonieris societatis populi et
duodecim bonorum virorum dicti Comunis deliberatione solempni et demum inter ipsos in
sufficientibus numeris congregatis in palatio
populi florentini premisso facto et celebrato
solempni et secreto scruptinio et obtempto partito ad fabas nigras et albas secundum ordinamenta dicti Comunis Eorum proprio motu pro
utilitate Comunis eiusdem Et omni via et more
quibus melius potuerunt prouiderunt et ordi-
nauerunt et deliberauerunt die vigesimoseptimo
mensis decembris Anno dominj Millesimo
quadragentesimo decimo nono Indictionis viij.
Quod Expensis Comunis florentie suum corpus
atque eiusdem exequie debeant in honorem dei
et famam sue felicis memorie honorarj Et pro
expensis dictarum exequiarum et pro dependentibus et connexis possint possint (sic) domini
priores artium et vexillifer Justitie populi et
comunis una cum officijs gonfalonieris societatis
populi et duodecim bonorum virorum dicti
Comunis et due partes ipsorum aliis etiam
absentibus et inrequisitis aut presentibus et
condecentibus motiuis aut remotis uel quolibet

Inpeditis stantiare et soluj facere cui et quibus et prout et sicut voluerint de pecunia deputata uel deputandum pro expensis capse casticorum dicti Comunis quid et quantum eisdem uidebitur et placebit Et quod Camerarius camere dicti Comunis teneantur et debeant de pecunia dicte capse casticorum dare et soluere recipere et habere debentibus pro dictis expensis uel aliqua earum seu alio cuicumque pro dando et soluendo predictas recipere debentibus quid et quantum per dictos dominos et eorum collegia aut duas partes ut quod fuit stantiatum et sine alia apodixa licentia stantiamento uel subscriptione habenda aut alia solepnitate seruanda et sine alia probatione uel actu uiso dumtaxat stantiamento predicto et sine aliqua retentione detractione uel diminutione alicuius diricture honoris aut gabelle si sic in stantiamento continebitur seu scriptum erit. Et quod illj intelligantur propterea recipere et haec debere quibus ipsi stantiauerunt seu quibus ille cui fuit stantiatum pro dando et soluendo eisdem dederit et soluerit etiam sine alia probatione uel actu.

Eo in predictas excepto et dumtaxat quod in uirtute presentis prouisionis non possit expendj seu stantiarj uel solui ultra florenos Trecentos aurej sed usque in dictam summam prout dominis et collegiis uisum fuerit seu placuerit.

Non obstantibus in predictis uel aliquo predictorum aliquibus legibus statutis ordinamentis prouisionibus aut reformationibus Consiliorum populi et comunis florentie obstaculis seu repugnantiis quibuscunque et quantuncunque derogatarij penalibus uel preactiis uel etiam si de eis uel ipsorum aliquo debuisset uel debetur fieri specialis mentio et expressio Quibus omnibus intelligatur et sit notificatum et expresse specialiter ac generaliter derogatum Et quod per predictas in hac presenti prouisione obtentas &c Vt super in prima prouisione huius consilij usque ad finem prouisionis eiusdem.

Quam quidem prouisionem domini Priores et vexillifer predicti vna cum officijjs gonfalonieris societatis populj et duodecim bonorum uirorum Comunis predicti Inuicem in sufficientibus numeris congregatis in palatio populi supradicto iudicauerunt cedere ad utilitatem euidenter Comunis eiusdem premisso et facto inter ipsos omnes solempni et secreto scruptinio et obtempto partito ad fabas nigras et albas secundum formam ordinatam dicti Comunis deliberauerunt

pro euidenti utilitate Comunis predicti proponi posse et super ea propositionem fieri etiam ipsam eadem die vigesimaseptima mensis decembris predicti In consilio populi Ciuitatis florentie.

Qua prouisione lecta et recitata ut supra dictum dominus propositus ut super omnia dictum est proposuit inter dictos consiliarios super dictam prouisionem et contentum in ea super qua petijt super omnia pro dicto Comunj et sub dicta forma bonum et utile Consilium Inpertirj Post que illico dicto proclamato in dicto Consilio per precones comunis eiusdem ut moris est quod quilibet volens uadat ad consulendum super prouisionem et propositam super dictam et nemine eunte et ipso proposito de voluntate consilio et Consensu offici dictorum dominorum et vexilliferi proponentis et petitum fauentis inter consiliarios dicti Consilii numero – CLxxxxj – presentium in dicto Consilio Quod cui placet et videtur supradictam prouisionem et contentum in ea procedere et admictendum tenere et admicti fierj obseruari et executionj mandari posse et debere et firma stabilitate tenere in omnibus et super omnia secundum formam ordinis dicti Comunis Et ipsorum Consiliarorum uoluntatibus exquisitis ad fabas nigras et albas ut moris est repertum fuit – CLvij – Ex ipsis Consiliarijs dedisse fabas nigras pro sic et sic secundum formam dicta prouisio obtenta firmata et reformata fuit non obstantibus reliquijs xxxiiij – Ex ipsis Consiliarijs repertis dedisse fabas albas in contrarium pro non'. f. 210v, ratified by 138 votes to 12 on 28 December (number present 150).

Document 3

FLORENCE, ARCHIVIO DI STATO, MEDICEO AVANTI IL PRINCIPATO, FILZA 5, NO. 958 LETTER FROM GIOVANNI DI BICCI DE' MEDICI TO MICHELE COSSA DATED 31 DECEMBER 1419.

'Io vi scrissj piu di sono / Il caso della morte del Chardinale & quanto lasciaua a Voj et quanto a Giouannj et quod d Giouanni glia adauere quando fio In eta dannj. xx. et manchando in questo tempo anno a venire a voj o a vostrj figli / Reda lascio e poveri iddio che fiano nominati per gli essechutorj / ancora comprendo la sustanza e si pocha che ritrattone la spese del mortoro fia faticoso potere dare compimento a leghati / Oltracio s apparechia tante persone a domandare sare faticoso Al papato poterli paghare et da hora hanno cominnato quellj dellj Spinj a farsi fare certi comandamentj a luditore della chamera cio e alli essechutorj che non paghino / siche brigha et faccenda sara assai / ancora I compagni et Io siamo disposti fare cio che sia possibile che quello che lascio abi effecto / Ne per ancora non vegho che vi si possa dare piu vno avviso che vn altro che per voi s auesse a ffare / Senone possendo mostrare che delli auessi auto o tratto del suo o vostro patrimonio in nanzi che fusse Chardinale o dipoi somma di danarj / arebbe molto a giouare a cannellare la ragione di chi a domanda et simile se voj potessj mostrare et cosi Giouanni che de ui douesse dare o essere stati damnificati per sua cagione / a colto / e doluto a ciascheduno Ciattadino la sua morte e grandissimo dico si grande honore glie stato fatto per la Signioria di quj che a nessuno signiore si potrebe fare maggiore / questj che domandono sono tuttj per debitj fattj nel tempo chelli era leghato di bolognia et poi che fu papa / Ancora pare che faenno pensiero in caso non potessono ottenere quj andare contro a voj et contro a glialtrj leghatarij che auessono preso / non so Io quanto di questo Vegnendo il caso voi lo stimasse / debbe essere costj di valentj huominj et non sarebe altro chutile averne in torno accio consiglio et a visarvj di quello vi paresse fosse vtile. Altro per ora non occorre di dire Christo sia vostra guarda in firenze adj xxxi di dicembre 1419.

Vostro G. de medici'

Document 4

FLORENCE, ARCHIVIO DI STATO,
MEDICEO AVANTI IL PRINCIPATO,
FILZA I, NO. 231
LETTER OF MICHELE COSSA TO
GIOVANNI DI BICCI DE' MEDICI,
DATED 25 JANUARY 1420.

'Egregie pater honorabilis post reccomandationem mercodi ad le xxiiij del presente mese ebi vna vostra lettera e tra laltre cose che scriuite, dite, che sono molte persone, s'aparecchano ad adomandare debiti, et in spetialita quelle di spini, et che loe fatto certo comando per lauditori della camera, che non debiate pagare, cioe ad li exequtorj. Di che molto m'inde marauiglio, che quello che non fero nella Vita della bene-

detta anima di mio zio labiano facto ad la morte: li fatti soi me credo certo, che tanto Voi, quanto li exequtorj, li deuano ben sapere, se luj avra debito, et se debito fece quando era legato ad bologna lo fe per adiutare la eclesia di dio, che quando ando legato come so certo che Voi sappiate ce mese delli denari soi piu che Vintimilia fiorini, et se debiti fese poi che fo papa similmente lo fe per la Ecclesia. Io so divero da persona che lu sa che poi che bolognia, se redusse ad stato populare, tutti li debiti che fese mio zio fo facto lassegnanto ad chi douia auere. et sepure fosse che luj avesse debito, noj non semo herede ad luj, questo si porria ben prouare per homini fiorentini e bolognesi, et forse voi et li exequtorj lo sapete, quando ello stette ad lo studio, ad noue ouero vndici anj che spese parecchi migliaia di fiorinj dello patrimonio suo et douerralo ben sapere Antonio di Jacopo del Vigna, che fo nel temppo di giacomino del gogio et di philippo di michele da Empoli, li qualj quando luy era ad lo studio pagauano li denari per parte di mio auo che li bisognauano. lo dampno che mio patre et laltrj mei zii et tutta la casa mia aue recepeuto non mistendo a scriuare, cha e noto non solamente per questo regame et per ytalia ma per tutto lo mondo che solamente di rendite, che avia mio patre et io, di sette Anni che stetti di fore mi peiorò piu di decimila fiorini, senza quello dellaltry mej zii e senza la roba che auemo venduta tanto quello che vendi misser Gaspare quanto quello che vendio misser Marino et quella che o uendita io che fu di mio patre, che monta bene altre tanti decimila fiorinj senza laltre spese che auemo facte dapoi che recuperamo la roba nostra come Voi sapete, che trovammo omne cosa sfatto et distrutto et ancora restamo in gran debito. Pertanto prego Voi et laltrj exequtorj ad che con la fede e la speranza mia et similmente di giouanni che Vi piaccia demostrare ad noi la bene che voleste ad la bona memoria del nostro zio et ancora per vostro honore come exequtore che sete, che Vi piaccia fareci dare li denarij li quali cialassati nostro tio secondo lo suo testamento, et ancora mandarci la copia dello testamento. se nulla persona poi che avaremo auutj li denari li sara fatta cagione sence adomandara nulla. Io per me et similmente per giouannj Vi pregamo che questi fatti tanto Voi quanto li compagni Vostri che Vogliate essere nostri defensori che noi non volemo ne avemo ad piatare con nullo che foria gran peccato poi che avemo perduta lo avere et semo rimasi disfatti per nostro tio che questo che ci lassa e per li dapni receputi per luy ad perdarilly. Io dico che tanto mio patre quanto io nabemo maj senon male e persi ad la morte aue fatto male ad me non so sia stata la cascion che ad me lassa cinquemilia fiorinj et ad giovanj decemilia questo non dico che me rincresca che ha lassati ad giouannj che voria che illauesse lassati piu. che io me doglio di quello che non ave facto ad me che o cinque figliolj traliquali no doi femine e ringratio Dio che non e per mio defecto che io non li fe maj vergogna so ad vostro piacero, scritta In Castro Ouo in napoli die xxv Januarij xiiiª Indict.

Vester filius michael cossa miles manu propria.'

Endorsed, 'Da Napoli a ij di febraio.'

Document 5

FLORENCE, ARCHIVIO DI STATO,
PROVVISIONI 110, f. 204r.–v.
27 JANUARY 1420/1

'Honorantia digiti Sancti Iohannis Batiste.

Secundo provisionem infrascriptam super infrascriptis omnibus et singulis deliberatam et factam per dictos dominos priores vexilliferum et gonfalonerios societatum populi et duodecim bonos viros Comunis Florentie secundum ordinamenta dicti Comunis, que talis est videlicet.

Cum die tertia decima presentis mensis Ianuarii fuerit ab ecclesia Sancte Marie de Angelis de Florentia ad ecclesiam Sancti Iohannis Batiste eiusdem civitatis dicitus index dextre manus eiusdem Sancti Iohannis Batiste, sing(u)laris defensoris ac patroni populi et comunis Florentie, reliquia quidem non solum toti populo Florentino cui idem Santus est caput et protector, verum etiam cuilibet christiano reverendissima pretiosissima et accepta donata eidem populo per felicis recordationis reverendissimum patrem et dominum, dominum Baldassarrem Coscia cardinalem Florentinum appellatum et nuper Santissimum in Christo patrem et dominum, dominum Iohannem papam vigesimum tertium, delatus omni populo florentino nec non dominis prioribus Artium et Vexillifero Iustitie dicti populi et comunis multa cum reverentia sociatus fueritque, pro huiusmodi translatione ob reverentiam Dei ac defensoris predicti, cuius predicta reliquia

pars corporis est, facte certe expense in cera, drappellonibus et aliis, et propterea sit, pro satisfaciendo habere debentibus, necessarium opportunam habere pecuniam. Ideo Magnifici et potentes domini, domini priores Artium et Vexillifer Iustitie populi et Comunis Florentie. . . . providerunt . . . die vigesimo septimo mensis Ianuarii predicti.

Quod camerarii camere comunis Florentie tam presentes quam futuri teneantur et debeant de pecunia deputata vel deputanda pro expensis capse generalis dicti Comunis dare et solvere fratri Iohanni Christofani, uno ex camerariis Camere armorum palatii populi Florentie, libras ottuaginta otto et soldos tredecim florenorum parvorum pro satisfaciendo habere debentibus pro dictis causis. . . .'

Agreed by Priori and Gonfaloniere, and on same day by the Consiglio, by 201 votes to 3.

Confirmation next day 'pro expensis factis in processione et honorantia digiti Sancti Iohannis Batiste' by 154 votes to 1 (*vol. cit.*, f. 207 r–v).

Document 6

FLORENCE, ARCHIVIO DI STATO,
MERCANTI DI CALIMARA,
DELIBERATIONE DALL' ANNO 1424 AL
1426
ff. 2–3 (in margin *scripta pro domino Baldassarre de florenis cccc*')
DIE XIIII FEBRUARII (1425/6).

'Prefati suprascripti Consules, excepto ditto Betto eorum collega absente, simul in domo ditte artis collegialiter congregati pro eorum uffitio exercendo, auditis Bartolomeo Valori et Cosma de Medicis Commissariis executoribus domini Baldassarris Cosse, dicentibus se indigere et eis expedit habere denarios pro expeditione seppulture que fieri faciunt pro corpore ditti domini Baldassarris, et aliunde percipere non possunt nisi ab arte seu opere Sancti Iohannis, videlicet de denariis quos ditta opera habuit ab eis in deposito, et propterea eisdem consulibus placebit providere quod ipsi possint habere et percipere de dicto deposito saltim usque in quantitatem florenorum quadringentorum.

Volentes ditti consules dittis executoribus et seu commissariis complacere ac etiam maxime quia aliter faciendum fieret contra ius et sine aliquo utile ditte artis et seu ditte opere, misso et fatto inter eos solepni et secreto scruptineo et obtento partito ad fabas nigras et albas, ut moris, deliberaverunt et stantiaverunt quod accipiantur et reassumantur ditti floreni quadringenti auri a Filippo Bernabe de Aleis et sociis et ab Antonio domini Niccolai de Rabatta et sociis, qui habent in depositum denarios predittos habitos a dittis executoribus, videlicet a quolibet eorum Filippi et Antonii floreni ducenti auri, et dentur Gu(c)cino de Sommaria depositario Opere, qui dentur et dari possint dittis commissariis et prout deliberaverunt et voluerunt.'

Document 7

FLORENCE, ARCHIVIO DI STATO, MERCANTI DI CALIMARA, DELIBERATIONE DALL' ANNO 1424 AL 1426
ff 10r–v. (in margin *'electio presbiterorum pro domino Baldassarre Cossa'*
DICTA DIE 11 (i.e. 2) MAY (1426).

'Suprascripti Consules omnes simul in ditta arte collegialiter congregati pro factis et negociis ditte artis una cum Niccolao Manovellozii, Adovardo Lodovici de Acciaiuolis et Bardo Francisci de Bardis, quos ad infrascripta deputaverunt in arrotos, et volentes, ut tenentur, ad executionem earum que pertinent ad eorum officium super fattis et negociis ultime voluntatis domini Baldassarris Cosse olim cardinalis et quondam pape Iohannis XXIII sepulti in ecclesiam Sancti Iohannis, et maxime ad electionem duorum presbiterorum qui singulis diebus pro anima ditti domini Baldassarris missam celebrent in dicta ecclesia: premisso tamen inter eos solepni et secreto scruptineo ad fabas nigras et albas, ut moris est, et obtento partito, providerunt ordinaverunt elegerunt et deputaverunt ac commiserunt honestis et providis viris

    presbitero Iacobo (*blank*) de Colle et
                        ad celebrandum
    presbitero Mariano (*blank*)

et quod celebrent missas et alia divina officia singulis diebus et horis debitis in dicta ecclesia pro anima ditti domini Baldassarris. Et quod eis et cuilibet eorum dentur et dari ac solvi possint nomine elemosine ut habeant unde se alimentare possint, quolibet mense quo serviverint in dittis missis et officiis, florenos duos auri pro quolibet

eorum, eisdem dandis et solvendis per depositarium pro arte Kallismale predicte, quarterii Sancti Iohannis.'

Appendix B

THE WILL OF CARDINAL RAINALDO BRANCACCIO

From Società Napoletana di Storia Patria, *Miscellanea, M.S. B.8, vol. xxvi, f. 58r–61v.*
ARCHIVO DI S. ANGELO A NILO

Copia estratta dall' incartamento 1, fol. ° 24 a 33.

Copia del testamento del Card. Rinaldo Brancaccio, fatto in Roma, nel suo domicilio presso S. Mª in Trastevere il 27 Marzo 1427

In nomᵉ d(omi)ni Amen. Anno a nativ(itat)e ejusdem millᵒ quadringᵒ vigesimo septimo, ind. V die vero (*word omitted*) Martis, pontificatus SS.ᵐⁱ in Chr.ᵒ patris & d(omi)ni n(ost)ri Martini divina providentia Pape V anno 10ᵒ, Universis et singulis presentem instrumenti paginam inspecturis tenore presentium fiat notum quod RR.ᵐᵘˢ in Christo Pater et dominus Raynaldus miseratione divina Sᵗⁱ Viti in Macello S.R.E. Diaconus Cardinalis de Brancatiis nuncupatus et mente tamen et discretione in ultimis attendens quod nil certius sit morte et incertius hora mortis, et quod semper ante oculos mentis remanens sit ultimus dies, volensque discretione durante disponere seriose pro tempore de iis, quae sibi a Domino sunt collata, ut audire mereatur verbum Sancte Scripture, 'Euge serve bone et fidelis' etc. Considerans quod verba Scripture, que ammonet novissima, ne videlicet Mundi huius fallacibus obblectamentis quis detentus, vitam, ad quam nos creavit Altissimus obliviscatur eternam, et quod in carne viventes difficile est eis se suaque disponere ante mortem, ut non indigeat corpore testamentorum, que

formamur post occasum aliqua exequenda re-
linquere, que aut humana fragilitas in vite
velocissimo cursu obmiserat, aut in . . . (*sic*)
nitas abvocabat de bonis suis, invocato auxilio
Redemptoris prius, condidit Testamentum: In
primis Animam suam recommendavit Altis-
simo Creatori, gloriosissime Virgini Marie, S.º
Michaeli Archangelo, Sº Joanni Baptistae, S.º
Joanni Evangeliste, SS. Apostolis Petro et Paulo
et Andree, Sanctisque Laurentio et Vito Marty-
ribus, ac toti Curie Sanctorum Civium caeles-
tium Superiorum.

Item cum Predecessores sui semper gesserint,
et ipse gerat devotionem ad Ordinem Fratrum
Predicatorum, et ex hoc construxerit, seu
deputaverit, et dotaverit unam Cappellam in
Ecclesia S. Dominici de Neapoli dicti ordinis,
voluit et elegit corpus suum ubicumque eum
decedere seu mori contigerit, ipsum ad dictam
Cappellam, vel ad Cappellam SS. Angeli et
Andree, ad Nidum, ubi dicti testatoris heredes
com bono consilio determinabunt portari, et
deferri, et ibi sepelliri quam cite fieri poterit,
Exequias autem suas fieri voluit supra foenum?
(sic. locum) juxta ritum Romane Curie pro
Cardinalibus consuetum de pecuniis et bonis
suis percipiendis per infrascriptos exequutores
seu fideicommissarios suos juxta eorum debitum,
quos rogat et hortatur in domino Jesu Christo ut
ab omni superfluitate et pompis abstineant et
dictas exequias fieri voluit si in urbe decederet,
in Ecclesia S. Mariae supra Minervam, vel apud
S. M.ªm Mayorem, cujus Archiprebyster est,
secundum quod suis exequutoribus videbitur, et
ubi fiant exequiae, recondatur corpus causa
depositionis, si alibi in principali Conventu Predicatorum ubi eum mori contigerit, et ibidem
corpus deponi transferendi Neapolim; Quod si
in loco obitus non esset aliquis conventus dicti
Ordinis, vel transferatur Corpus et exequiae ad
aliquem honestum et vicinum locum dicti
Ordinis, vel expediantur omnia in principali
Ecclesia loci obitus, si ipsis exequutoribus visum
fuerit expedire, translationem tamen sui corporis
ad Neapolim semper firmum tamen voluit
dictus testator quod in dicta Cappella, vel in alia
Hospitalis SS. Angeli et Andree ponatur sepultura, quam dictus testator fecit fieri, per manus
Cosmi de Medicis et Bartolomei de Bardis, et
detur dictae Cappellae unus pannus seu Cortina
aurea more Dominorum Cardinalium, et pro

quibus reliquit pecuniam necessariam recipien-
dam de bonis suis.

Item voluit et ordinavit dictus Testator, quod in
Cappella sua predicta singulis diebus continuis
temporibus celebrentur tres Misse per fratres
dictis Ordinis, vel deputandos ab eis, una ad
honorem B. Virg. Marie, alia pro Anima sua et
suorum et aliorum Defunctorum, qui dotaverunt
beneficia, que ipse Testator possidet. Tertia sit
secundum devotionem celebrantis, ita tamen
quod sexta feria ipsa tertia Missa celebretur
semper de S. Cruce; voluit etiam quod in dicta
Cappella ardeat semper diu noctuque lampa
accensa ante imaginem B. M. Virginis et quod
singulis annis diei obitus sui fiat Anniversarium
per fratres dicti Conventus pro Anima sua pro
quibus videlicet et missis, lampade, et Anniver-
sario provisum et satisfactum est per ipsum
testatorem dicto Conventui S. Dominici Neapolitani, ut patet ex Instrumento celebrato et
publicato in Civitate Aversana per Notarium
Petrillum Bulcanum, quod Instrumentum dictus
testator in observationem, et defensionem pre-
missorum in omnibus voluit et per omnia observari et contenta in d.º Instrum.º attendere, ad
quem ipse testator se refert.

Item voluit et ordinavit quod tota familia sua,
que presens fuerit in exequiis ipsius Testatoris
induatur panno nigro pro qualitate statuum, et
tredecim pauperes, quorum una sit femina,
induantur panno albo juxta arbitrium exequutorum, et quod dicte Familie et pauperibus
administrentur necessaria victus ut prius.

Item voluit et ordinavit dictus Testator quod
Familiaribus suis, quibus est promissum salarium, sit eis satisfactum factoque prius computo
de summa quam restarent habere, illis autem
quibus non fuit salarium promissum qui
(tenuerunt?) habueruntque pro grato intrare
domum suam dicentes quod nihil habere vole-
bant si officiales ipsi non fuerint, provideatur eis
de aliqua subventione pro arbitrio exequutorum,
ante quam redeant de domo.

Item reliquit et voluit ipse testator quod die
sequenti post obitum suum duo vel tres sacerdotes incipiant Missas S. Gregorii etc. . . . (*sic*)
florenos auri tres.

Item reliquit pro aliis missis celebrandis et
elemosynis erogandis etc. florenos auri centum . . .

Item reliquit pro maritagio duarum vel trium Virginum . . . florenos auri centum.

Item reliquit Hospitali S. Spiritus in Saxia vel Urbe pro uno Calice florenos auri viginti.

Item reliquit Ecclesie B. Marie Majoris de Urbe pro uno Calice florenos auri trigintaquinque etc.

Item reliquit B. M.ᵉ in Transtyberim alios vigintiquinque Florenos auri ut supra.

Item reliquit Ecclesie S. Viti in Macello de Urbe pro reparatione aut evidenti alia utilitate flor. auri Vigintiquinque ut supra.

Item reliquit eccl. Sabine de Urbe florenos auri 25 etc.

Item reliquit Monasterio S. Sixti de Urbe fl. aur. 15.

Item reliquit ecclesiae S. Falconis Nidi Neapolitani uncias quinque.

Item reliquit Cappelle S. Viti fundate et ordinate in Ecclesia S. Dominici Neapolis et alie in Hospitali SS. Angeli et Andree ad Nidum omnia paramenta persone sue, cujuscumque coloris et forme, et etiam alia que habet in Domo sua et in cappella domus ipsius testatoris juste pro medietate, videlicet ac omnia paramenta spectantia ad ecclesias dividendas inter dictas cappellas juste pro medietate, videlicet uni cappelle unam medietatem et alteri cappelle aliam medietatem.

Item reliquit Domino nostro Martino meliores Mulum et bestiam Mulam vel equos quos habet.

Item reliquit Fusco Brancatio Nepoti suo ducentos florenos auri de Camera.

Item reliquit Andree Brancatio Consobrino domini Joannis de Brancatiis florenos sexcentos, etc.

Item reliquit dictus testator quod executio hujus presentis sue ultime voluntatis fiat per exequutores.

Item voluit quod dicentibus se debere recipere ab eodem . . . sit eis satisfactum infra biennium etc.

Item voluit quod infrascripti exequutores statim recipiant propria auctoritate de bonis mobilibus etc.

Item reliquit dicte Cappelle Hospitalis tres

planetas, quas pro eadem fieri fecit, que sunt adhuc apud Sartorem . . . (sic) nec non Crucem argenteam ipsius testatoris et Thuribulum pulchrum cum navicula et breviarium in quo ipse Testator dicebat officium, Missale parvum et librum divinorum Officiorum, que omnia sunt in domo ipsius etc.

Item reliquit domino Paulo Nepoti suo Cameram suam laboratam cum hominibus et duabus viridi et albi coloris.

Item Domino Ioanni altero nepoti suo Cameram suam rubeam novam.

Item Fusco nepoti suo Cameram suam antiquam, qua utitur modo et unam Mulam vel equum.

Item reliquit domino Joanni Abati de Positano unam Cappam.

Item reliquit domino Bartolomeo Abati Monasterii S. Marie Rotunde ut emat unam cappam.

Item reliquit domino Antonello de S. Bartolommeo unam cappam.

Item reliquit Paulo Scaura et Honofrio ejus fratri 50 florenos etc.

Item voluit et ordinavit quod Hospitale S. Andree, quod est in platea Nidi reedificetur cum omnibus locis, officinis et horto necessariis et utilibus et quod in eo fiat Altare sive Capella sub vocabulo SS. Angeli et Andree, in qua capella fiat precise divinum officium ut super describitur, in Capella sua in Ecclesia Fratrum Predicatorum; et quod presbyteri inibi eligendi sint et admittentur, revocentur ad voluntatem Rectorum ipsius Hospitalis, et quod in dicto Hospitali fiant lecti cum parteriis ordinati, et fulciti in numero tresdecim, duodecim pro pauperibus et unum pro Hospitalerio, et pro dicti hospitalis, et Cappelle completione et aliorum necessariorum reliquit in numerata pecunia quinque milia florenos auri de camera.

Item voluit et ordinavit quod pro usu et substentatione dicti Hospitalis et pauperum ibidem affluentium emantur in locis vacuis tot possessiones et bona, quod valor annuus, qui provenerit ex fructibus possessionum que jam empte sunt, uncie quadraginta octo, et alique terre.

Item voluit et ordinavit quod Universitas Nobilium platee Nidi habeat eligere quolibet anno duos nobiles de dicta Platea, quorum unus sit semper de Domo de Brancacciis, quorum duorum eligendorum anno finito expiret Officium, et alii duo eligantur, qui duo sic electi habeant regere, gubernare et dispensare dictum Hospitale et ejus bona et pro eis agere et experiri ac vendere, ac introitu(m) dictorum possessionum et exitu(m) annotare et scribere, ut possint clarum computum reddere, quem computum nulli omnino teneantur ponere vel reddere, nisi dumtaxat Nobilibus dicte Platee, vel quibus ipsi Nobiles deputaverint, possintque dicti duo electi ad eorum nutum et voluntatem instituere et removere Hospitalerium et Sacerdotes dicti Hospitalis, ita quod gratia super hoc per Sanctissimum dominum Papam concessa in omnibus et per omnia observetur, et prout in literis ipsius domini Testatoris desuper confectis et sugillo suo munitis plenius continetur et habetur.

Item dedit et legavit domino Paulo nepoti suo 1000 florenos auri pro maritagio filie sue.

Item voluit ipse testator quod si quis heredum suorum quidquam de Domo sua violenter contra aliorum exequutorum voluntatem reciperet, ipso facto careat hereditate et omnium sibi per eumdem dominum testatorem legatorum.

Item Cappelle S. Angeli et Andree reliquit unam Conam suam cum multis reliquiis.

Item reliquit eidem cappelle omnia tappeta sua.

Item dixit quod vina greca que sunt penes Bartholomeum de Bardis sunt domini Pauli Brancatii nepotis sui etc.

Item reliquit Andree de Brancatiis Breviarium quod fuit domini Episcopi Tudertini et omnes libros qui fuerunt quondam domini Nicolai de Senatibus litterarum Apostolicarum Scriptoris.

Item reliquit Marie de Brancatiis de panno nigro tantum, quod se possit induere more Neapolitano.

Item voluit quod nihil possit fieri in exequutione testamenti sine deliberatione et ordinatione Reverendissimi domini Cardinalis Novariensis.

Item dixit qualiter Mattheus Benedicti Curie romane debet sibi dare has pecunias, de quibus voluit emi unum Missale de 16 florenis aureis pro Monasterio S. Sabe.

Item librum Evangeliorum copertum coreo viridi legavit Cappelle et unam campanellam de metallo.

Item reliquit Ecclesie S. Joannis Lateranensis 25 florenos auri etc.

Item reliquit 4 Candelabra argentea magna dicte Cappelle SS. Angeli et Andree.

Item dixit Reverendus Pater dominus Cardinalis testator presente Cosmo de Medicis, qualiter apud ipsum Cosmum adest quedam cedula sex millium florenorum auri de Camera, de quibus voluit compleri Cappellam et Hospitale prediciti, et voluit quod Cappella pulcherrime depingatur quod sit Cappella domini Artusii et Magistri Antonij de Pennis et quod in eodem fierent fenestre de vitro et ferro.

Item voluit quod emantur tot possessiones, que omni anno responderent duas uncias Carolenorum pro suppletione fundationis dicti Hospitalis non obstantibus aliquibus terris que supersint.

Item voluit ut ematur una terra arbustata pro vino ad usum pauperum et servitorum Cappelle et Hospitalis.

Item voluit quod Campane emantur pro ipsa Cappella.

Item voluit quod ponantur in eodem Hospitali sexdecim lectos bene fulciti cum copertoriis et linteaminibus duplicibus, et ulterius omnia necessaria ipsi Capelle et Hospitali emantur, Scanna, Listas, Bancos, Capsas, strameta pro conservatione rerum et bonorum Hospitalis et Cappelle predictorum.

Item voluit quod si quid remaneret de dictis 6000 florenis, quod illud restitueretur integraliter suis heredibus.

Item reliquit Cappelle sue unum par ambullarum de argento.

Item omnia jocalia Monasterio S. Sabine. Crux, mitra, et alia quecunque et omnes et singule scripture et privilegia ad ipsum Monasterium spectantia, dicto Monasterio tradantur et assignentur.

Item voluit quod pars horti, que spectat ad ecclesiam B. Marie Transtyberim restituatur Canonicis ipsius Ecclesie sine contradictione.

Item recommendat exequutoribus suis . . . (*sic*) Viros magistros Aloisium et Antonium Medicos suos.

Item quod corpora quondam Ponelli et Philippi nepotum suorum cum corpore suo simul Neapolim transportentur si commode fieri poterit.

Item reliquit Cappelle SS. Angeli et Andree horologium magnum de 24 viginti quatuor horis.

Item dictus dominus testator ultra omnia legata, legavit er ordinavit dicto Hospitali SS. Angeli et Andree tria milia ducatos, videlicet mille quadringentos octaginta duos quos posse habere manualiter Bartholomaeus de Bardis Mercator, prout in Cedola dicti Bartholomei plenius continetur, et mille quingentos decem et octo extrahendos, elevandos et recolligendos de juribus beneficiorum et Cappelle dicti testatoris, hoc adjecto quod vult quod extrahatur de parte hereditatis contingentis Dominum Joannellum de Brancaciis nepotem suum tantum, qui quidem tria millia ducati voluit et mandavit assignari et dari Nobilibus Platee Nidi, qui Nobiles una cum domino Paulo de Brancaciis Milite Nepote suo emant possessiones pro dicto suo hospitali.

Item voluit et ordinavit quod omnia emolumenta sive jura Cappelle, que debebuntur sibi tempore obitus sui vel post, deveniant ad manus Cosmi et Laurentii de Medicis Mercatorum de Florentia etc. prout in litteris Domini nostri Martini Pape etc.

In omnibus tamen bonis suis paternis et maternis stabilibus mobilibus etc instituit sibi universales heredes Dominum Paulum militem et Joanellum de Brancatiis nepotes suos etc.

Exequutores autem, seu Fideicommissarios hujus presentis Testamenti, dictus Testator esse voluit et reliquit Reverendissimus in Christo Patres Dominos Lauderi et SS. Cosmi et Damiani S.R.E. Cardinales dominos Paulum de Juvenatis, Paulum et Joanellum de Brancatiis et Fuscum de Brancatiis, et Joannem Abatem de Positano, Fr. Thomam Priorem S. Sabine et Joannem de Medicis de florentia etc.

Acta fuerunt hec Rome in domibus solite residencie dicti domini Cardinalis testatoris, site apud S. Mariam Transtyberim, sub anno, indictione, die, mense et Pontificatu quibus supra, presentibus ibidem reverendissimo in Christo

patre Gentile, episcopo Suessano, nec non magnifico viro domino Poncasio Montis Odorosii Comite, Venerabilibus ac Religiosis Viris Joanne Beate Marie de Positano Amelphitani Diocesis, et Bartolommeo Beate Marie Rotunde extra muros Ravennatenses Ordinis S. Benedicti Monasteriorum Abatibus. Magistris Theologie Paulo de Valle, Aloisio Mutiliani, Antonio de Surmontis Medico, Antonio de S. Bartolommeo Archidiacono Vulturianense et Paulo Scaura Laico Neapolitano testibus ad premissa vocatis specialiter et rogatis.

Extracta est presens copia ab alia copia sistente in Archivio Venerabilis Ecclesie et Hospitalis SS. Angeli et Andree ad Nidum, et proprie in volumine primo Scripturarum dicte nobilis Ecclesie, quod conservatur in Scansia III dicti Archivi.

Appendix C

Document 1

THE LETTER OF GIROLAMO ALEOTTI

FROM VIRGIL GADDI I IN BIBLIOTECA MEDICEO-LAURENZIANA, ff. 211v–213r, WITH PRELIMINARY NOTE ADDED FOR MESSER CORRADO BELLARMINO OF MONTEPULCIANO, PROBABLY *c*. 1462

'Leonardus Aretinus scripserat contra optimum et prudentissimum virum bartholonmeum politianum secretarium apostolicum iam uita functum, ut apparet in uolumine epistolarum ipsius Leonardi.

Eam epistolam quum ieronimus aretinus legeret permotus rei indingintate ac turpitudine scripsit contra leonardum suppresso tamen eius nomine. Scripsit autem ad pogium uirum doctissimum et disertissimum, curia eugenii Pontificis demorante Florentiae.

Pogius ipsam ieronimi epistolam legendam obtulit aurispae cincio blondo karolo aretino doctissimis uiris et secretariis apostolicis qui omnes dingnis conuitiis leonardum affectum fuisse cum risu et iocho asseuerabant obconuitia et maledicta que false et iniuste in bartholonmeum politianum defunctum impegerat.

Hieronimus aretinus clarissimo et disertissimo pogio. Vt facile coniicies exconsuetudine mea, que mihi tecum intercedet frequentissima si uoles. sum exingenio uerecundior atque subtimidus. ea de causa si quempiam amo, si cuiusque uirtutes et ornamenta contemplor. nequeo coram aut uiri uirtutem aut amorem meum ad integrum explicare. ne forte ueniam insuspitionem adulationis quam et si licteris semper sum cautissime detestatus. nescio quo id pacto eueniat, ut fidentius securius que id calamis quam lingua persequar siquis est mihi non immerito laudandus, ut quodam modo uideatur epistola minus erubescere minus que in se habere suspitionis. Tua vero laus pogi clarissime adeo illustris est, certa fixa et fuse late que uulgata, ut nemo illam repetens assentationis suspitionem ulla ex parte subuereri debeat. Nec tam enim qui te extollit, blanditor censiri potest quam qui a laudibus tuis temperat, summa negentia (*sic*) at que sordida seu certe nequitia praeditus dum id rite assequi ualeat. Proinde mi pogi angor cura non facili quod ea non sum copia neque ingenio ut possim uel uirtutis uel ornamentorum tuorum particulas exigere. Ita que hoc onus te laudandi in eos rei(*ci*)iam qui ista uberius commodius que posse uidentur. Meum erit in te tantum admirari peritiam licterarum tritam atque reconditam concinnitatem orationis, dicendi elegantiam, et grauitatem miro quodam modo festiuitati orationis admixtam. quibus rebus eruditissimorum iuditio omnes nostrae huius aetatis homines facile superas. Deinde humanissimam naturam tuam, qua plane mea sententia non modo aetatis nostre sed omnium pene retro actorum seculorum hominibus superior extas. quanta me enim excepisti humanitate primo et proximo die si tamen diei partem crepusculum dicimus. O letabilem mihi diem seu noctem appellare mauis qua primum pogio agressus sum. Quam te mihi affabilem tractabilem que prebuisti, ut si me multos annos familiariter utereris, nil (*cer*)te supra conari debuisses quam tuo illo primo congressu fecisti mihi plane gratissimo et iocundissimo. Quod si istarum utra vis perse aut eximia licterarum peritia aut singularis humanitas hominem laude dingnum efficit, quanto excellentius ambe coeuntes at que connexe istuc ipsum obtinebunt. Et mea quidem semper fuit sententia pluris esse fatiendam sine licteris humanitatem quam sine humanitate licteras.

Vnde paucis retro diebus facete iocatus sum. Cum amicus quidam atque ipse spatiaremur ad diue marie templum. daretur que nobis forte obuiam unus inter doctissimos a plerisque habitus precipuus lento pede et graui passu adueniens, dixisset que mihi socius adesse uirum clarissimum et qui nouit egregie in homines invehere maxime uita functos, ego dissimulato illo pertransii nullum uenerationis et consuetae obserua(*n*)tie ritum ad ortus. Interrogatus a socio quamobrem licteratissimo uiro et mihi probe agnito uerticem nihil mandassem. Abeat dixi in malam rem nec sibi nec licteris suis inuideo. Nam rite est asinus ab omni offitio et humanitate abhorrens. Itaque mi pogi tanti facio modestiam et humanitatem ut ea sine quamvis multas licteras floccipendam, sine uero licteris eam ipsam et admirari et uenerari soleam. Tu si aliter sentis facile cedam tibi nec ero in errore pertinax. At ea ipsa duo simul iugata et in uno homine concreta uirum faciunt ex homine admirabilem atque omni laude dingnum. Eiusmodi uiros semper ego apuero obseruaui totoque desiderio amplexus sum. qualem te modo nactum esse mihi ipsi gratulor mirifice. fido enim pro tua illa ingenua humanissima que natura me tibi non recusatum iri. Si me ita que adscribes unum in tuis filiis, non uereor oppinione tua ullo tempore frustaberis (*sic*). Vale felix colendissime pater ac domine 1439.'

Document 2

F. FABIANO BENCI, FAMIGLIE RIGUARDEUOLI DI MONTEPULCIANO, COPY BY GIUSEPPE FRANCESCHI, 1723, MS. IN ARCHIVIO CAPITOLARE, DUOMO, MONTEPULCIANO

'Aragazzi III

La Famiglia degl' Aragazzi di MPulciano, che faceua per sua Impresa tre Teste di Ceruo, come uedeasi nel celebre sepolcro di marmo di m.ʳ Bartolomeo, fatto nella Pieue di S. Maria della Patria nostra, oggi Chiesa Cattedrale; ed al presente si uede nella Facciata del nostro S. Agostino, ebbe principio, come sotto, da

(*folio 94—The Aragazzi Family Tree follows here: see page opposite*)

Questa Famiglia mancò nel trascorso secolo, è antica e fù nobile. Jacomo di Bartolomeo di Mʳ

THE ARAGAZZI FAMILY

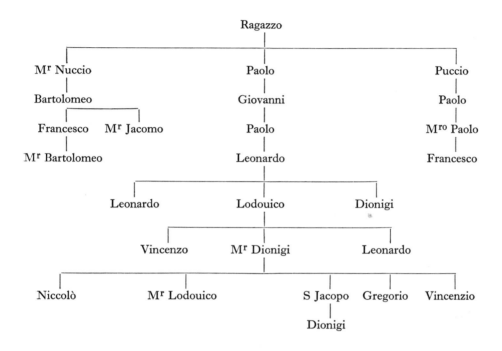

Nuccio fu Arciprete di MPulciano nell' anno 1400. Dionigi di Leonardo oltre l'essere Arciprete nella nostra Pieue, fu eletto Vescouo, e prima d'esserne inuestito mori. Vincenzio di M^{ro} Dionigi pronipote dell' accennato Dionigi fù pure Arciprete nella Patria nel 1541. à tempo di cui Marcello Ceruini all' ora Cardinale, e poi Papa come Commissario Apostolico di Paolo III. diè al Capitolo di MPulciano le Costituzioni proprie. Mr Bartolomeo poi di Francesco di Bartolomeo principale splendore di questa Famiglia merita al suo luogo Elogio particolare, ad esso dunque rimettramo (*sic*) il cortese Lettore. Deuesi notare come il sud.⁰ Giacomo di Bartolomeo di Mr Nuccio Arciprete di MPulciano, trouasi nelle antiche memorie appresso i Sig.^{ri} Conti Ceruini, auer ottenuto da Bonifacio IX. l'anno 1400. sotto il di 9. Aprile l'uso delle Insegne Vescouali Mitra, e Bacolo, et il priuilegio di ordinare ad quatuor minores Ordines colla sottrazione dalla Juridizione del Vescouo di Arezzo, la quale fu sempre controuersa à nostri Arcipreti.'

Document 3

FLORENCE, ARCHIVIO DI STATO,
CATASTO 219, f. 229r

Questo e il catastro e sustanze di me Francesco di Bartolomeo di messer Nuccio da Montepulciano, del terziero di Santa Maria e contrada di San Donato, asegniato questo dì XXVIII di febraio di comandamento degli uficiali del catastro ad Aldobrandino di Giorgio podestà di Montepulciano.

† Adi XXVIII di febraio 1428

Sustanze di Francescho di Bartolomeo della chontrada di San Donato, del terziere di Santa Maria, le quali rechò detto dì a me Aldobrandino di Giorgio d'Aldobrandino del Nero, al presente podestà di Montepulciano.

(at bottom, note as follows)
àsi a mandare, s'è bisongno, per Angnolo Ispinelgli.

f. 229v
(Note added by Don Battista, Priore della Parcia on 15 January 1430 [style *a nativitate*])

Di quanto ène scritto di questo e quello che rimase dele sustantie di messer Bartolomeio di

Francesco suo padre e quelli vogl[i]ono se ne faccia e a chiareza di ciò io dorni [*sic.* don] Baptista di Giovanni, priore di Sancto Pietro dalla Parcia, nepote di detto Francesco e di misser Batrolomeio (*sic*) mio cugino, fo fede di quanto è scritto, e a chiareza di ciò òne fata questa scritura di mia propia mano in Montepulciano, questo dì 15 di giennaio 1430, in presentia d'Antonio di Piero da Fiore[n]ze e Giovanni del (*sic*) Salvadore del Caccia e scrivani degli oficiali del catastro.

f. 230r
Francescho di Bartholomeo di misser Nuccio da Montepulciano, della contrada di Sancto Donato, allibrato nella decta terra e contrada, à gli infrascripti beni. E prima.

Una casa posta in Montepulciano, nella sopradecta contrada di Sancto Donato, allato le cose di Salinbene di Pietro et le cose delle heredi di Iohanni di Rossello. Et sotto la detta casa una cella che r(i)esce apiè el saxo et via di Comuno dalle due parti. Extimata   Lire CCC XXX

Marginal annotation: questa casa è ove abitiamo co' la famiglia.

Item à una casa et bottigha nella Mercantia et contrada di Talosa, allato le cose di Meio di Francescho di Christofano et le cose delle heredi di Benedecto di Micchele tengono i frati di Sancto Domenicho, et via di Comuno dinanti et dirieto, et via vicinale. Extimata   Lire CLXXX

Àsene l'anno di pigione da Nicholò di Papi di Mano lire dodici l'anno.   Lire XII

Item à una casa posta nella contrada di Voltaia, allato le cose del decto Francescho et le cose di Nanni di Reda et le cose delle heredi di Fofo di Fuccio et via di Comuno. Extimata
        L. LXXX

Àsene l'anno di pigione da Micheleagnolo da Siena lire dieci   L. X

Item à una parte d'una casa posta nella decta contrada di Voltaia, allato le cose del decto Francescho et le cose delle heredi di Fofo di Fuccio dalle due parti et via di Comuno dalle due parti. Extimata lire   LX

Àsene l'anno di pigione da Fucc(i)o di Fofo lire tre.   Lire III

Item à una casella posta sulla decta contrada di Voltaia, dirieto a casa di Guasparre di Niccholò dalla Noccha et via di Comuno. Extimata

Lire XX

Àsene l'anno di pigione da Scharamucc(i)a da Perugia lire cinque.   L. V

Item à una casa con una piazuola dirieto, posta nella contrada di Collazi allato le cose di Christofano da Fighini et via di Comune. Extimata

L. XV

Àsene l'anno di pigione da Nani di ser Marcho lire cinque.   L. V

Item à uno casalino a orto, posto nella contrada di Sancto Donato, allato le cose di ser Niccholò di Paulo di Guccio et le cose di Francescho di Pietro di Casuccio et l'orto di Bartolomeo di ser Niccholò et via di Comune da due lati. Extimata

L. XV

Il detto chasellino è uno orto a uso della chasa, che nulla se ne trae.

Item à una vigna che si chiama gl'Appostuli, allato le cose del decto Francescho et le cose de'frieri di Sancto Iohanni et le cose della pieve di Sancta Maria et le cose d'Agni(o)lo di Iohanni decto Bottazo et via di Comuno, verso Pisinano, et le cose delli heredi di Nanni di Tommassino. La quale è staia tredici di vigna et uno staio di terra. Extimata per tutto   L. V^c (= 500)

Richolglio in mia parte barili venti di vino; olio metadelle venti.

f. 230v.

Item à uno pezo di terra lavoratia, posta nella contrada degl' Apostoli et di Fonte Castello, allato le cose del decto Francescho et le cose di Agni(o)lo di Iohanni decto Bottazo et la via che va a Fonte Castello et via vicinale. La quale è staia quatro e mezo. Extimata   L. LXXV

Àsene l'ano per nostra parte staia quindici—

Item à uno pezo di terra lavoratia, posta nella contrada di Valardegni, allato le cose della pieve di Sancta Maria et heredi di Salvestro di Paulo di Goro et heredi di Giacopo di Ciano et via di Comuno. La quale è staia cinque et quarti uno. Extimata   L. CXV

Àsene l'anno di fitto da Fa . . . (?)ro di Salvestro di Ghoro, l'ano, lire V.   L. V

Item à uno pezo di terra vignata e lavoratia posta nella contrada di Poggio Mancino presso le tombe de' Giuderi, allato le cose di Nardo di Francescho et le cose di Andreia di Christofano et le cose di Cenni del Magnano et via di Comuno. La quale è staia quatro. Extimata

L. LX

Àsene nostra parte barilli quatro di vino; grano staia due —

Item à uno pezo di terra lavoratia, con uno staio di vigna, posto nella contrada di Sanelle, longo le cose di Francescho di Pietro di Casino et le cose d'Antonio di Min(i)ato et le cose d'Agni(o)lo della Pieve. La quale è staia sei. Extimata   L. XLVIII

Àsene di fitto l'ano d'Angnolo della Pieve f. uno l'anno.

Item à uno pezo di terra vignata et lavoratia, con uno palazuolo sopra essa esistente, posto nella contrada si Sancto Cervagio allato le cose che fuoro di monna Orne et oggi del decto Francescho e'l Sanctarello di Sancto Cervagio et via di Comuno dalle due parti. La quale è staia nove. Extimata   L. CLXXV

Àsene i' nostra parte staia centosesanta.
Olio metadelle ventiquatro.
Biada staia sesanta.

Item à uno pezo di terra vignata e lavoratia, posta nella decta contrada allato le cose delle heredi di misser Antonio di misser Currado e le cose di Francesco di Ghezo dalle due parti, et le cose delle suore di Sancta Chiara et Antonio del Testa et via di Comuno. La quale è staia quindici. Extimata   L. CCLXX

Vino barili sedici.
Zafferano libre due.

f. 231r

Item à el decto Francescho di Bartholomeo uno pezo di terra lavoratia et soda, che fu del podere di Grande speziale, posta nella contrada di Sancto Cervagio allato le cose di monna Petra, donna fu d'Alberto di Iohanni et le cose di Coletta di Tommaxo da San Germano et via di Comuno e'l fossato. La quale è staia trenta. Extimata   L. CCX

Marginal annotation: intendesi detto pezo cho' detti 2 pezi da San Cerbagio.

Item à uno pezo di terra soda, posta nella contrada di Colonelle, che ci fu già uno palazuolo, allato le cose che fuoro d'Agostino di Lucha et via di Comuno dalle due parti. La quale è staia diciotto. Extimata   L. VIIII

Marginal annotation: intendesi col detto podere di San Gervasio.

Item à uno pezo di terra sodo, fu del Salvaticho, allato le cose di Nanni di Mencuccio et le cose di Stefano di Bianchuccio et heredi di Pietro di Ceccharone. La quale è staia quatro. Extimata
                                        L. VI

Marginal annotation: intendesi col detto podere di San Cervagio.

Item à uno pezo di terra lavoratia, posto nella contrada di Norviano, allato le cose delle heredi di Nino di Gionta dal Monte e'l fossato di Ragazone. La quale è staia quindici. Extimata
                                        L. XLV

Marginal annotation: intendesi col detto podere da San Cervagio.

Item à uno pezo di terra posto nella contrada di Colonnelle, allato le cose delle heredi d'Agni(o)lo di Christofano di Iohanni di Cone e'l fossato. La quale è staia vintiedue. Extimata   L. LXX

Marginal annotation: intendesi col detto podere di san Cervagio.

Item à uno pezzo di terra sodo et murecce, posto nella contrada di Colonelle allato le cose di Christofano di Iohanni di Cone et le cose delle heredi di Mino di Gionta dal Monte et le cose delle heredi di Ceccho da Chiucio e'l fossato di Colonelle et di Fognano. La quale è staia ottantadue. Extimata   L. XXX

Marginal annotation: intendesi col detto podere et non si lavora.

Item uno pezo di terra lavoratia, posto nelle pertinentie della villa dela Strada, allato le cose di monna Filippa di Iacopo spetiale et heredi d'Andreia di Iohanni di Ciolo e'l Salarcho e sodi d'Artimone. La quale è staia vintocto. Extimata
                                        L. LVI

Queste sono sei partite che sono sei pezi di terra chome seghuita, posti nella villa della Strada. Àsene i' nostra parte staia cinquanta.

f. 231v

Item à el decto Francescho di Bartholomeo uno pezo di terra posto nelle pertinentie della villa

dela Strada, allato le cose di Pietro d'Agni(o)lo di ser Niccholò et le cose che fuoro d'Antonio di Menchinello et via di Comuno e'l Salarcho. La quale è staia trenta. Extimata   L. LX

Item à uno pezo di terra sodo apiè il podere di Checco di Ghezo, allato le cose delle suore di Sancta Agnese et via di Comuno. La quale è staia octo. Extimata   L. IIII

Item uno pezo di terra in duoi volture, posta nel poggio d'Artimone, allato le cose d'Andreia di Iohanni di Ciolo et le cose di Domenicho di Nuto e'l Salarcho. La quale è staia sette. Extimata
                                        L. XI

Item à uno pezo di terra posto nella decta villa della Strada, allato le cose di Niccholò di Paulo di Suaga et le cose di Pietro d'Agni[o]lo di ser Niccholò et via di Comuno La quale è staia tre. Extimata   L. VIII

Item à uno casalino posto nella decta villa, allato le cose di Pietro d'Agni(o)lo di ser Niccholò dalle due parti et via di Comuno dalle due parti. La quale è staia mezo. Extimata   L. III

Item à uno pezo di terra a oliveto et alcuna vite, posto nella contrada di Sancto Iohanni volta vecchia, allato le cose di Giovanni Grosso et le cose di Domenicho di Capanna et le cose di Lorenzo Tromba et le cose di Iacopo del Riccio et via di Comuno. La quale è staia quatro. Extimata   L. XXXVI

Abiane i' nostra parte metadelle trentasei d'olio. Vino nonulla –

Item à uno pezo di terra vignata, posta nella contrada di Marchiena, allato le cose di Tommaxo di Iacopo e frati di Santo Domenicho e via di Comuno. La quale è staia tre. Extimata
                                        L. XXXVI

Abianne l'anno i' nostra parte barili tre di vino.

Item à uno mulino a acqua, posto ala Parcia allato la gualchiera di Nardo di Cenni et le cose della badia di Petroio et via di Comuno, con staia di terra. Extimato   L. CXXX

Àsene l'anno di fitto da Santi di Domenico mugnaio staia sesanta di grano.

f. 232r

Item à el decto Francescho di Bartholomeo uno pezo di terra parte vignata e parte lavoratia, posto nella contrada di Peschaia allato le cose di maestro Piero da Milano, sartore, et hercedi di ser Neri di Vannuccio et via di Comuno dalle due parti. La quale è staia sette. Extimata   L. CXL

Abiane l'anno i'nostra parte staia venti di grano; vino, barili quatordici di vino.

Item uno pezo di terra alla badia Arniano in due volture nel piano del Salarcho, allato le cose di monna Francescha di ser Lionarolo et heredi di Duccio di Paruta et Lencio di Viva et via di Comuno. La quale è staia diciotto. Extimata
L. L

Abiane l'anno i' nostra parte staia cinquanta di grano, mettendo queste 3 partite leghate insieme.

Item à uno pezo di terra, posto nella decta villa allato le cose di Lucha d'Andreia et heredi di Benedetto di Micchele et Nuccio di Guerrino et via di Comuno. La quale è staia dodici. Extimata
L. XVIII

Item à uno pezo di terra nella decta via, nel piano del Rigo, allato le cose di Crociano di Paulo et heredi di Iohanni di Farsetto et la chiesa di San Grappaldo. La quale è staiora sei. Extimata
L. XII

Item uno mezo podere posto a Villanuova per non divixo con le heredi di Salvestro di Paulo di Goro, allato le cose di Antonio di Petrino et Domenicho di Cino. È la sua parte staia trenta, sodo. Extimato
L. XV

Istà sodo e non se n'à nulla.

Item uno pezo di terra nelle pertinentie della badia Argnano, luogo decto Fontanelle, allato le cose di Crociano di Paulo et Iohanni di Pietro dal Monte et via. La quale e staia otto. Extimata
L. XVI

Item uno pezo di terra sodo e macchie, posto nella villa di Castelvecchio si chiama el campo del Morone, allato la chiesa di Castelvecchio, et altri sodi. La quale è staia sei. Extimata L. III

Àsene l'anno di fitto per fieno grossi 3.

Item uno pezo di terra vignata, posta nella contrada di Fognano, allato le cose della Capella di Sancta Agata et Nanni d'Agni(o)luccio et via di Comuno. La quale è staia due. Extimata
L. XX

Àsene l'ano i' nostra parte barili cinque di vino.

f. 232v

Item à uno pezo di terra vignata et lavoratia, posta nella contrada di Sancto Cervagio allato le cose del decto Francescho et le cose di Paulo di Iohanni di Nuto et via di Comuno dalle due parti. La quale è staia quatro o circha. Extimata
L. L

Àsene i'nostra parte l'anno barili cinque di vino: grano staia dieci.

E più comprai io Francescho di Bartolomeo di messer Nuccio da Montepulciano della contrada di San Donato, del 1416, una possesione parte vigna e parte terra, la quale è circa dieci staia, presso a Siena a uno miglio, nella contrada detta Poggio di Reggio, comune di Santo Emiliano, alato ala via del comune et Bernabò d'Agnolo di detto luogo et il monistero d'Ognisanti et il fossato, per prezo di fiorini setantasei d'oro sanesi. La quale possesione comprai per dare a ghodere, mentre che ssi vive, a monna Balda figliola fu de ser Francescho Naldi da Siena et mia sirochia consubrina, perchè essa mi fece carta di donazione inter vivo(s) d'una casa dove essa abita. La quale casa è posta in Siena, nel terziero di Santo Martino, nella contrada et compagnia di Rialto et Cartagine, alato Mino di Paolo da Monterone et maestro Martino di Bartolomeo, dipintore da Siena. La quale casa (word missing, a?) et dinanzi et dirieto la via del Comune. La quale casa et possesione deba fruttare la detta monna Balda tutto il tempo dela sua vita, poi deba rimanere a me overo ale mie rede. Nonn ò alchuno frutto. Voglio avervi avisato d'ogni mia cosa.

f. 233r

Al nome di Dio, adì XXII di febraio 1428

Qui a piè faremo richordo di tutti i beni mobili di me Francescho di Bartolomeo di misser Nuccio da Montepulciano, dela contrada di San Donato, come apiè per ordine diro.

In primo asegnio avere in soccio con Agnoluccio di Maria et Tofano et Viva et Paolo suoi figl(i)uoli, setanta fra vache, ginici et giovenchi; et le dette vache ànno ventisei vitelli dietro, che le diedi per sei anni in soccio, e in capo di sei anni le dobiamo partire per mezo. Fece dì 4 di dicembre passato tre anni che l'ebono, che ànno ghuadagnato il quarto di detto bestiame, et i tre quarti rimanghono a me. Siamo stati insieme e ragioniamo che tucte le dette bestie vagliano fiorini trecentocinquanta, che sono i tre quarti f. dugentosesantadue e mezo.

E più ànno di mio i detti Agnolucio e figl(i)uoli nel contado di Montepulciano, nella villa d'Aquaviva, quatro fra cavalle e polle(d)re, ch'al principio costaro f. quindici, e cosi debo ritrar prima io. Et sicondo pare a lloro, ora tucte vagliono fiorini trentacinque, che ne tocha a mme f. venticinque.

E più debo avere da detti Agnoluccio et figl(i)uoli per più cabelle paghate per le bestie et altre cose anno àuto da me in danari contanti f. venti-quatro soldi tre di moneta fiorentina.

E più à di mio Nanni del Peza e Pietro suo figl(i)uolo, miei lavoratori al mio podere di San Cervagio nel contado di Montepulciano, presso ala tera a mezo migl(i)o, ànno cinque buoi, stimati f. quarantacinque.

E più ànno due polledre asinine, stimate f. quatordici.

E più debbo avere da lloro, prestati contanti, f. venticinque s. sei danari dicesette di moneta fiorentina.

E più debo avere da Dinuccio di Ghuerrino e da Andrea suo figliolo, miei lavoratori ala Strada, contado di Montepulciano, f. diciotto, de' quali loro m'anno sodo sula loro capanna ala Strada con quatro staia di terra, e loro la frutano.

E più à di mio il sopradetto Dinucio di Ghuerino e Andrea suo figl(i)uolo, miei lavoratori ala Strada, contadi di Montepulciano, tre buoi i quali gli sono rimasi per fiorini trentatre e tre quarti perchè se ne scortichò uno.

E più à di mio una puledra asinina per f. nove.

E più tiene da me Nanni di Nuccio dala Strada ventotto pechore. Credo vagl(i)ano fiorini mezo l'una.

E più comprai da Biagio di Cenni sei porci fra maschi e femine, tielli alla Parcia, contado di Montepulciano, costaro f. tre e f. uno gli prestai.

E più ò col Cianpaolo ala badia Arniano uno bue che costò f. sette e mezo, lavora mecho terr(e)no.

E più tiene da me una bestia asinina femina, costò f. tre.

De danari contanti ò a ffare conto con Filipo di Bernaba e Domenicho e compangni. De' quali quando arò fatto conto, notificherò ala Signoria vostra di quanto a me restano a dare, et farollo

ala venuta d'Aldobrandino di Giorgio, nostro podestà.

Dipoi per non sentirmi sano, non potendo venire con Aldobrandino, ò diliberato scrivere quello ch'io credo avere avere da Filipo e Domenicho di Bernaba degli Agli e compagni, che pocho penso vi sia dal più o meno, e credo sieno f. dumila. I quali son quelli sopr' a' quali io vivo di spese di comune di Firenze e di Montepulciano, vestire, calzare e le al(t)re e altre cose che acagiono di spese.

E più debo avere in Firenze da Ghuiglielmo di Giunta f. cento quarantanove e soldi – , i quali sono per resto di panni fiorentini li vendei, che n'è ora il termine.

De' detti danari sono debitore ad Antonia mia figl(i)uola, donna fu di Mariotto di Conte d'Arezo, f. trecento cinquanta, de' quali n'à scritta di mia mano. Lo resto, fino a f. cinquecento che fu la sua dota, ne fu contenta lei da Michele di Conte d'Arezo, fratello di Mariotto suo marito. Si chè a me viene a restare miei propri f. milleottocento –

ff. 234r

Qui dapiè farò ricordo io Francescho, dele persone ch'io ò a governare.

> Prima la persona mia, d'età d'anni 64 o circha
> l'arciprete mio fratello, d'età anni 80, infermo
> monna Ghabriella mia sirocchia carnale, d'età 75 anni, vechia e inferma
> la donna mia, d'età d'anni 25
> tre fanciulle femine, dele quali ne sono due a balia
> una fante che mi costa f. 8 l'ano
> uno fante che mi costa f. 12 l'anno
> uno ronzino al'uso mio

E più asegno avere ad avere da Nanni del Peza e Pietro suo figl(i)olo, miei lavoratori a San Cervagio, staia novanta di grano.

E più debo avere da Dinucio e Andrea suo fig(i)uolo, miei lavoratori ala Strada, staia cento-venticinque di grano prestato.

E più ò in casa mia staia circha staia (*sic*) trecento di grano, del quale come che abia boce di soldi cinque lo staio, non se ne troverebe tre, e se non fosse i danari contanti mi truovo, di che io ò qualche provedigione, per grano et per vino non potrei vivere.

f. 234v

† 1429

Dipoi che Francescho di Bartolomeo diè il chatasto, morì messer Bartolomeo suo figl(i)uolo in Chorte di Roma, ch'era chericho e segretario del Santo Padre, adì XXVI di giugnio e fè suo testamento cho' licenzia del Santo Padre e lasciò sua reda universale il sopradetto Francescho suo padre. E le sustanzie sue e gli charichi farò richordo qui dapiè.

Una chasa posta in Roma, allato alla chiesa di Santo Apostolo

Una vicchia (*sic* vigna) posta i' Roma, alato a San Gianno (*sic*)

Ritrassesi da Chosimo de' Medici & Cⁱ di Roma ducati 1200

Ritrassesi da Francescho degli Alberti & Cⁱ di Roma duc. 1300

Ritrassesi dal detto Francescho degli Alberti per più arienti a lui venduti in Roma   duc. 497

Ritrassesi di danari contanti se gli trovorono in chasa in fiorini di più ragioni, trovati oculti nella vicchia e in chaso (*sic*) e nella chassa
                                                        duc. 4696

E più si trovò in una borsa XXI anella, in parte d'oro e d'ariento, di stima   duc. 100

E più in vasella d'ariento, pesò libre 38, di stima di f. 8 libra, monta   duc. 300

E più le maserizie di chasa, chom'ese(re) letta, libry e ornamenti di chamera e panni lini e lani, di stima   duc. 1000

E più 3 muli, tra maschi e femine   duc. 50

E più 4 chavagli   duc. 60

9203

E più s'asengnia dicati treciento, e quali (*canc.* lasò) diè il detto misser Bartolomeio a mona Antonia sua sorella, e dipuoi Fra(n)cescho pa(d)re della detta monna Antonia gli prese lui e rimasonsi in lui   duc. 300

Incharichi

Una chasa posta i' Roma, dove il detto messer Bartolomeo abitava, che ll'à tolta il papa

Una vicchia posta i' Roma, che se l'è tolta il papa per sè

Lasciò per testamento f. 400 di camera a maritare fanciulle   duc. 400

Lascia alla ghapella sua, che vi stia e chapellani e dotala duc. 600   duc. 600

Lascia a'frati degli Agnoli di Firenze duc. 100

Lascia al munistero di Santo Aleso di Roma
                                                        duc. 100

Lascia si facci dire 500 mese e diesi grossi uno per una   duc. 15

Lascia al chardinale di San Marcello duc. 500, che gli abbi a stribuire per Dio chome a lui pare
                                                        duc. 500

Lascia a' suo famigli di chasa duc. 200
                                                        duc. 200

Lascia a mess. Agnolo da Montepulciano duc. 100   duc. 100

Lascia f. 200 a 2 sue nipote, per aiuto della dote loro   duc. 200

Lascia f. 60 di camera per vestire poveri e per asequio chome piacerà a frate Lupo duc. 60

Laschia che se facci una sepultura in Montepulciano, che l'aveva data a fare a sua vita, che chosterà duc. 1000 quando sarà condotta qui
                                                        duc. 1000

f. 235r   Incharichi detti di mess. B.

Ispesesi per fare l'asequio suo a Roma e rechare il chorpo suo qui, in tutto si spese duc. 300, e vestiti   duc. 300

E più per una lapide si fè là, duc. XXI
                                                        duc. 21

3591

Di poi piaque a Dio chiamare a sè la benedetta anima di Francescho, padre del detto messer Bartolomeo, adì 29 di settembre 1429, e fè suo testamento e lasciò ereda messer Iachopo suo fratello charnale, ch'è arciprete di Montepulciano. E fè questi leghati, chome apreso si dirà.

Lascia a monna Tita sua donna f. 800 per le dote sue   f. 800

Lascia a tre sue fanc[i]ulle femine, quando si mariteranno, f. 700 per una   f. 2100

Lascia che si facci tre paia di paramenti da chiesa   f. 550

Lascia a' frati di Santo Aghostino per murare la chiesa di Montepulciano   f. 1600

Lascia a' frati di Santo Domenicho per murare una chiesa di santo Lucha di Montepulciano   f. 600

Lascia a' frati di San Giovanni del Pog(i)uolo   f. 50

Lascia alla chiesa di Santa Maria Maddalena, ch'è in sul monte Charcianese   f. 200

Lascia alla chiesa di San Lorenzo di Montepulciano f. dieci   f. 10

Lascia alla compagnia di Santo Istefano della detta terra, si chiama la compagnia de' grandi, X chape   f. 5

Lascia alla compagnia della Vergine Maria di de(tto)luogho, X chape (e) uno letto fornito   f. 15

Lascia alla chiesa di Santa Lucia di detto luogho   f. 10

Lascia alla chiesa di San Biagio fuori delle mura   f. 20

Lascia (a) 2 figl(i)uole d'Anguolo di Ricc(i)o   f. 40

Lascia a monna Ghita a monna Ghita (sic) suo figl(i)uola e dona di Papi di Nanni per supra alla sua dote   f. 350

Lascia a monna Antonia sua figl(i)uola e dona fu di Mariotto di Conte f. 200   f. 200

Lascia ad Angnolo Spinelli uno Dante et una mula.   f. 30

Lascia a monna Ghita e monna Antonia suo figl(i)uole   f. 12

Chostò il mortorio e lla (in)fermità del sopradetto Francescho   f. 250

f. 235v

Terra di Montepulciano. Fran° di Bartolomeo di mess. Nuccio. Terziere di Santa Maria.
Adi 4 d'aprile 1430 per diliberazione degli (u)ficiagli del chatasto anulorno l'agiunta a(ve)va datta adì 26 di gienaio 1429, perchè come beni venutti dipoi dette la schrita al chatasto, e però non s'à a mettere nè a sustanze nè a incharicho di detta agiuntta.

         Messa a libro, c. 136

FLORENCE, ARCHIVIO DI STATO, CATASTO 257 (CAMPIONI DEL DISTRETTO MONTEPULCIANO E VALIANO)
MARGINAL ANNOTATION ON f. 137v, REFERRING TO THE MONEY DEPOSITED BY FRANCESCO ARAGAZZI WITH FILIPPO DI BERNABÒ DEGLI AGLI

Disse don Batista e Angniolo Spinegli che saldorono poi il chonto e trovoron v'aveasi in detto dì f. dumillasesantatre chomputandovi drento f. 149 di Ghuglielmo di Giunta.   f. 2136

Document 4

FLORENCE, ARCHIVIO DI STATO, CARTE STROZZI-UGUCCIONI, 3ª SERIE, FILZA 132

BRIEF OF MARTIN V, WRITTEN BY BARTOLOMMEO ARAGAZZI, TO GIOVANNI DE' MEDICI, 16 NOVEMBER 1428

     Martinus pp. V

Dilecte fili Salutationem et apostolicam benedictionem. Cum multa quotidie nostre fragilitatis exempla in oculis nostris appareant / vnum hic nouissime factum est nobis et tibi dolendum / quod sine lacrimis referre non possumus. Nam tuus ille fidelis nosterque dilectus filius Bartolomeus de Bardis cum decem diebus grauibus oppressus febribus egrotasset / accelerata morte migrauit ad dominum / de cuius obitu doluimus et dolemus / non quia mali aliquid illi acciderit / qui in flore etatis sue ad beatorum vitam translatus est / et ad meliorem patriam reuocatus / sed quia dolorem tuum propter caritatem nostram erga te non possumus non sentire / fuit enim vir ille magne prudencie experiencie et virtutis / in quo tali viro amisso iacturam non exiguam senciemus / et tu fili dilecte plurimum perdidisti / Nam singulari affectu fide et diligencia nostra et tua omnia sibi commissa negocia administrabat / et singulari studio procurabat / amplitudinem et honorem tuum. Sed hunc casum paciente ferre debemus, et quecumque deo placita sunt equis animis tolerare. Hortamur itaque prudenciam tuam ut feras equo animo voluntatem dei, et cum illum semper in uita ut filium tuum dilexeris, hoc sibi unum praestes in morte / ut nulla afficiaris tristicia / sed pro anima eius ores / que non re-

quirit a te lacrimas nec dolores / sed pias elemosinas et oraciones ad deum / Nam cum optima disposicione et contricione ex hac uita discessit / ut sperare merito debeamus anime sue salutem. Ceterum indubie teneas fili dilecte quod honorem et statum tuum et societatis tue in Romana Curia et ubicumque poterimus / sicut hactenus cognoscere potuisti pristina caritate habebimus in omnibus occurrentibus rebus cordialiter recommissos / etiam si solum unus ex minimis tuis institoribus ad tuarum rerum custodiam remansisset / nosti enim singularem affectionem et beniuolentiam nostram erga te et tuos omnes, quorem honores et commoda libenter omni tempore procuramus. dat. Rome apud Sanctos Apostolos sub Anulo piscatoris die xvj Novembris pontificatus nostri Anno Vndecimo
B. de Montepoliciano
Endorsed Dilecto filio Nobili viro Johanni de Medicis Ciuj et Mercatori florentino.

Document 5

FLORENCE, ARCHIVIO DI STATO, NOTARILE ANTECOSIMINIANO, N. 96 (SER NICCOLÒ DI ANGELO NICOLAI, 1430–1434), *c.* 33r
6 DECEMBER 1430

procuratio domini Iacobi archipresbiteri

Antedictis anno, indictione et pontificatu, die VI mensis decembris. Actum in Montepoliziano, in domo infrascripti domini archipresbiteri, presentibus Nicolao Iacopi Mini et Petro Antonii Smachi de dicta terra, testibus ad hec vocatis et habitis.

Universis pateat manifeste quod venerabilis vir dominus Iacobus Bartholomei, archipresbiterus plebis Sancte Marie de dicta terra, non revocando aliquem suum procuratorem sed potius confirmando, fecit constituit ordinavit atque creavit suum dicti constituentis verum legittimum et indubitatum procuratorem etc. ser Barnabam Betti Iohannis alias Razi de dicta terra, absentem tanquem presentem, ad lites et causas etc. Item ad citaciones, proclamationes testium, sequestra, bannimenta, exbannimenta, requisitiones, protestationes, subastationes et omnes et singulos actus oportunos et necessarios in predictis et circa ea. Item ad capiendum accipiendum et nanciscendum omnes et singulas

tenutas etc. Item ad iurandum subspectum quemlibet debitorem et faciendum capi et detineri et exinde facere relaxari etc. Item ad substituendum etc. Et generaliter ad omnia et singula etc. Dans et concedens etc. cum promissione de rato etc., cum relevatione honeris fideiussionis etc. sub obligatione bonorum etc.

Document 6a

FLORENCE, ARCHIVIO DI STATO, NOTARILE ANTECOS, N. 96/IV (1430–34), p. 112, SER NICCOLÒ DI ANGELO NICOLAI, NOTAIO, p. 17
1430, 11 SEPTEMBER

Refutatio pro domino archipresbitero.

Predictis anno indictione et pontificatu die XI mensis settembris. Actum in monte policiano in domo domini Jacobi archipresbiterj dicte terre presentibus nanne bartolomej naldini guilielmo nicolaj et don batista johannis de dicta terra testibus ad hec uocatis et habitis. Vniversis pateat manifeste quod Jacopus minj angelj de dicta terra fecit domino Jacobo bartholomei archipresbitero plebis sancte marie heredi francisci bartholomej suj fratris heredis domini bartolomej franciscj finem refutationem transactionem et pactum de ulterius non petendo de quantitate settuaginta quinque florenorum auri in quibus dictus dominus Jacobus heres predictus tenebatur et obligatus erat vigore depositi facti per dictum Jacobum dicto olim domino bartolommeo et relicti in testamento francisci predicti dicto Jacopo. Et hoc ideo fecit dictus Jacobus quia fuit confessus tacitus et contentus habuisse et recepisse a dicto domino Jacobo herede predicto. Et quia habuit et recepit a dicto domino Jacobo florenos xxxj aurj pro residuo dicte quantitatis adsolvens et liberans dictum dominum Jacobum heredem predictum de dicta quantitate lxxv florenorum &c. Et promisit et convenit dictus Jacobus dicto domino Jacobo &c dictam refutationem liberationem et omnia et singula suprascripta perpetuo firma et rata habere tenere observare &c sub pena duplj dicte quantitatis &c cum refectione dampni et expensarum &c sub ypoteca et obligatione sui et suorum bonorum &c renuntians &c. Jurans et guaratizans &c. testibus

Document 6b

FLORENCE, ARCHIVIO DI STATO
N. 96/IV, f. 63
1431, 14 JUNE

Electio rectorum et sindici fraternitatis plebis sancte marie – actum in montepoliziano in coro ecclesie plebis sancte marie presentibus . . . Vniversis pateat manifeste quod Convocatis congregatis et coadunatis in coro ecclesie plebis sancte marie de dicta terra Venerabili viro domino batista johannis vicario venerabilis viri domini Jacobi Bartolomej archipresbiterj plebis sancte marie prefate . . . f. 64 Don batista Johannis pauli vicarius dominj Jacobi archipresbiterj dicte plebis sancte marie . . .

Document 7

MONTEPULCIANO, ARCHIVIO
LIBER REFORMATIONUM, 1433–7,
f. 249r
21 SEPTEMBER 1435

Et primo cum per potestatem civitatis Florentie molestati fuerunt et sint heredes et bona hereditatis Francisci Bartholomey quibus donnus Baptistas petat suis sumptibus unum oratorem transmicti Florentiam ad tuendum iura hereditatis et nostri Comunis, cum talis congnitio ad potestatem civitatis Florentie non pertineat vigore nostrorum capitolorum, ideo provideatur in predictis et omne aliud quod Florentie fieri deberet pro Comuni ut dictis consiliis placuerit generaliter proponendo.

LIBER REFORMATIONUM, 1433–7, f. 250r

Quod eligatur orator sumptibus donni Baptiste
Blaxius Datini, unus ex consiliariis dicti consilii, aringando consuluit super dicta prima proposita quod domini priores auctoritate presentis consilii possint eligere sumptibus dicti donni Baptiste unum oratorem qui Florentiam vadat ad tuendum iura dicte hereditatis et nostri Comunis, cui oratori detur notula per eos conficienda circa opus suum et omne aliud quod eis utile videbitur pro Comuni cum credentiarum litteris opportunis.

Document 8

LIBER REFORMATIONUM, 1433–7, f. 328
8 MAY 1436

Die octavo mensis maii suprascripti
Notula suprascriptorum electorum oratoribus
Magnifici domini priores (et) vexillifer populi una cum dictis eorum honorabilibus collegiis in dicta sala magna ut supra congregati, advertentes et considerantes tempus requirere oratores Comunis ut supra per eos electi, eant Florentiam, quare opus est eis dandam conficere notulam, vigore commissionis eis in predictis concesse ut supra, dato misso et obtento partito inter eos secundum Comunis ordinamenta, ordinaverunt ac fecerunt notulam infrascriptam dictis oratoribus dandam et per eos exequendam tenoris infrascripti, videlicet.
Imprimis credentiarum litteris magnificis et potentibus dominis nostris presentatis hanc eorum devotissimam Comunitatem recomictetis, preterea quod petatis quod per eos Magnificos et potentes dominos nostros ut opus erit et cum effectu provideatur quod sentente late per eorum potestatem civitatis Florentie contra hereditatem et bona hereditatis Francisci Bartholomey de Montepoliciano ad petitionem cuiusdam mercatoris de Marca, et similiter omnis processus formatus et seu condepnatio lata dicta de causa, revocentur, irritentur et cassentur, cum iurisdictionem nullam habeat in hac terra et eius comitatu dictus potestas vel alius, preter quam potestas huius terre eorum civis secundum capitula et pacta inita et facta inter eorum magnificam comunitatem et hanc eorum devotissimam comunitatem, allegando et obstendendo omnia capitula et iura huius comunitatis et dicte hereditatis necessaria et opportuna. Hoc expresse declarato quod nullam remissionem de predictis in aliquam personam cuiuscumque dignitatis vel status existeret faciatis, sed ut supra dictum est capitula nobis semper observata ab eorum comunitate effectualiter observari petatis in defensionem iurisdictionis nostre et iurium dicte hereditatis.

Document 9

REGISTRUM LITTERARUM
(COPIALETTERA 2). NO FOLIATION
9 JUNE 1436

Magnifici et potentissimi patres et domini nostri

singularissimi. Per la lectera della magnificentia vostra a noi mandata, inteso aviamo come di nuovo quelli da fermo stati sono ala vostra Magnifica Signoria per cagione dela sententia altra volta costì ottenero nela loro corte del podestà contro ali beni di Francesco di Bartholomeo nostro terrazano. Il perche la magnificentia vostra se intenta e vuole che di nuovo per noi si mandi a mostrare perche cagione detta sententia non merita executione. Il perchè ala vostra Magnifica Signoria per le presenti significhiamo che come mai per cosa nessuna ci diviamo dala volontà sua, così al presente e sempre per lo avenire fare intendiamo. Manderemo costà prestamente nostri ambasiadori ala magnificentia vostra a mostrare di nuovo esser iustamente stato fatto quanto neli proximi dì passati si fè per la nostra Magnifica Signoria insieme co' li nostri honorandissimi collegii in conservatione dele ragioni di questo nostro devotissimo popolo, el quale humilmente ala magnificentia vostra si racomanda. Parati semper vestre Magnifice dominationis parere mandatis. Datum in terra Montispolitiani, VIIII Iunii 1436.

Document 10

LIBER REFORMATIONUM, 1433–7, f. 331r
11 JUNE 1436

In eterni Dey nomine amen. Anno Domini ab eius salutifera nativitate MCCCCXXXsexto, indictione XIIII, die vero undecimo mensis Iunii.

Magnifici domini priores et vexillifer populi terre Montispolitiani una cum eorum honorabilibus collegiis numeris sufficientibus in sala magna antiqui palatii eorum Comunis pro factis dicti eorum Comunis utiliter peragendis congregati, servatis servandis, ordinaverunt deliberaverunt ac fecerunt propositas infrascriptas ad opportuna eorum Comunis consilia mictendas, videlicet.

Et primo cum magnifici et potentes domini nostri Florentini nostro scripserunt Comuni quod ad eos Florentiam mictatur qui obstentat qualiter sententie late per potestatem civitatis Florentie ad petitionem illius de Marca contra bona hereditatis Francisci Bartholomey non mereantur executionem ex quo necessarium est ad eos mictere qui iura Comunis et dicte hereditatis obstendat. Ideo in Dei nomine provi-

deatur in predictis et aliis si qua alia peragenda Florentie forent pro Comuni ut dictis consiliis placuerit generaliter proponendo.

Document 11

LIBER REFORMATIONUM, 1433–7, f. 400v
17 MAY 1437

Die XVII mensis maii suprascripti

Magnifici domini priores et vexillifer populi terre Montispolitiani una cum omnibus eorum honorabilibus collegiis in saletta congregati, obtento partito inter eos secundum Comunis ordinamenta, ordinaverunt ac fecerunt propositam infrascriptam ad opportuna consilia dicte terre mictendam.

Cum vigore litterarum magnificorum dominorum nostrorum transmissarum nostro spectabili potestati per eius curiam, Caterina filia olim Francisci Bartholomey Bartholomey (sic) fuerit capta et in custodia data domine Caterine Duccii Parute et domine Antonie filie eius ad petitionem et instantiam magnificorum dominorum nostrorum et dicti domini nostri potestatis. Ideo in Dey nomine provideatur in predictis ut dictis consiliis generaliter placuerit.

Document 12

LIBER REFORMATIONUM, 1433–7,
ff. 401v–402r
17 MAY 1437
COMMISSION TO SER GIOVANNI DI
BARTOLOMMEO DI NALDINO, SENT AS
'ORATORE' TO FLORENCE

Rappresenterai la lettera de la credentia a magnifici et excelsi nostri signori humilmente ala loro M^ca S. questa loro devotissima comunità raccommanderaj dipoi ala loro excelsa signoria significheraj come per lo nostro spectabile podestà per vigore de la lettera de la loro Signoria e stata presa la Caterina, figliuola fu del dilettissimo nostro terrieri Francesco di Bartholomeo et di casa il marito cavata in altra casa e stata messa et in custodia data, la quale cosa non piccola admiratione et perturbatione à dato a tutto questo loro devotissimo popolo. Il perché con ogni istantissima affectione si prega la loro excelsa Signoria che detta fanciulla faccia licentiare et al suo marito rendere et non farla trarre di questa terra, considerato che la intentione del padre fu che qui si maritasse et stesse et il suo tio il simile per testamento lassò, significando di parte in parte come le cose sono passate intorno a cciò, allegando quelle chiare, vere et autentiche ragioni richiede la materia, operando co' la loro Signoria con ogni istantia che la fanciulla per onore et utile di questa terra sia licentiata et qui rimanga, come è dovere et è di volere qui di tutti i suoi parenti et di tutto questo loro fedelissimo popolo.

Document 13

COPIALETTERA 3, f. 10r
JUNE 1437

Magnificis dominis nostris

Magnifici et excelsi atque gloriosissimi domini nostri singularissimi. Con debita riverentia adi due del presente dala vostra excelsa Signoria ricevemo lettera, per la quale volentieri avere inteso et exaudito il nostro ambasiadore intorno ala liberatione dela figliuola di Francesco di Bartholomeo nostro terriero, a noi per la vostra usata benignità significare degnasti, ala quale per la presente rispondiamo. La propria iustitia, benignità et gratia expectavamo, ricevuto aviamo dala vostra excelsa Signoria, la quale sempre a noi benignissima et gratiosa in ciascuno caso per lo quale a lei siamo ricorsi trovati aviamo, et per vera experientia sempre veduto quanta sia stata la fede, diletione et amore che essa ha portato a questo suo divotissimo et fedelissimo popolo. Il quale benchà a lui impossibile sia co' la mente concepere et per consequens colla penna expremere quante et quante esser deno le gratie et laude è obligato rendere ala vostra Magnifica Signoria et a tutto il vostro Magnifico popolo. Nientedimeno satisfacendo al presente con quello è a lui possibile, con istantissima affettione, riverentia et divotione, quanto sa et può ringratia la vostra gloriosissima Signoria, confidandosi sempre per l'opere mostrare quanta sia la fede, divotione et deli benifitii ricevuti obligatione in exaltatione dela vostra vittoriosissima Signoria, la quale felicissima et supprema a tutte l'altre meritamente desideremo et desideriamo. Contiene inter cetera detta vostra lettera, per fare ragione et tor via ogni controversia, la vostra Signoria avere intorno a cciò voluto procedere non per modo rigido nè indiscreto se forse per lo nostro podestà si fusse trasandato etc. Il perchè per noi ala vostra excelsa Signoria si risponde dala vostra Magnifica Signoria non essere mai proceduto nè potere procedere se non iustitia, per la quale tutti li suoi popoli rettamente sono governati et intese le informationi ala vostra Magnifica Signoria date, per far ragione non aver di meno potuto fare veramente comprendiamo. Et perchè alquanto dubitiamo che la parte non abbi gravato il caso in graveza del nostro spectabile podestà, sperando più di facili suo contento avere, per la presente vi significhiamo come esso humanissimamente si portò in mandare il suo cavalieri con tre donzelli per la fanciulla, la quale accompagnata dala sua suocera e da molte altre donne del vicinato dal detto cavalieri chiamate, honestissimamente condusse et essa lassò nela casa per li nostri anticessori diputata, sotto la custodia di due vedove honestissime donne, a detta fanciulla parenti. Onde se alcuna infamia a lui fusse stata data, per la presente, in testimonio dela verità significhiamo essere non vera ala vostra Magnifica Signoria, ala quale humilmente ci racomandiamo. Parati sempre vestre Magnifice dominationis parere mandatis. Datum etc. die VII Iunii 1437.

Document 14

COPIALETTERA 3, f. 17v
12 SEPTEMBER 1437

Magnificis dominis nostris

Magnifici et potentissimi domini nostri singularissimi. Ricorre con divotione e grandissima fede ala vostra excelsa Signoria il venerabile huomo don Batista, priore dela badia di S. Pietro dell'ordine di Valembrosa, nostro dilettissimo terriero, ad impetrare aiuto e favore mediante il quale Michelozo . . . intagliatore, vostro ciptadino, venga a fornire una certa cappella et sepultura di marmo del famosissimo nostro terriero messer Bartholomeo di Francesco, al detto Michelozo allogata et per llui principiata. Come da esso don Batista piena informatione aver potra la vostra Magnifica Signoria, la quale istantissimamente preghiamo presti al detto don Batista il suo usato favore, mediante il quale la volontà d'esso messer Bartholomeo, che così lassò per testamento, sia adimpiuta. Tale opera sara pietosa e a Dio accepta. Et per essa obligati rimaremo ala vostra excelsa signoria, ala quale humilmente sempre ci racomandiamo. Parati semper vestre Magnifice ac victoriosissime dominationis obbedire mandatis. Datum in terra Montispolitiani XII septembris MCCCCXXX-septimo.

Document 15

COPIALETTERE
31 MARCH 1438

Magnificis dominis nostris

Magnifici et potentes domini nostri singularis-simi etc. Ricorre ala vostra Magnifica Signoria monna Cristofana di Checho di Berto, nostra dilecta terriera, ad impetrare dala vostra excelsa Signoria aiuto et fauore, per lo quale essa sia satisfatta di fiorini venti, i quali debba avere per la sua figliuola dala heredità di Francesco di Bartholomeo, per lo passato nostro honorevole terrazano, sequendo il testamento di messer Bartolomeo suo figliuolo. il quale per testamento lassò fiorini quattrocento per l'amore di Dio, i quali si dessino a alquante fanciulle quando si maritassino. Fra le quali pare che esso Francesco nominasse la figliuola dela detta mona Christo-fana per fiorini venti, come da lei piena informa-tione aver potrà la vostra Magnifica Signoria. Et perche la heredità di detto Francesco è pervenuta in donno Batista, nostro terriero, priore dela Parcia, il quale è del' ordine di Valinbrosa, i detti lasciti non si pagano perche allega non potere essere gravato se non con licentia del' abate di Valinbrosa, suo superiore. Il perche da iustitia, misericordia et pietà commossi, la detta monna Christofana et l'altre povere et miserabili fanciulle ale quali detto lascito appartiene, ala vostra Magnifica Signoria racomandiamo, essa con istantissima affectione pregando degni provedere che per lo abate si conceda licentia che per detta cagione detto donno Batista possi essere gravato qui dali nostro podestà, a' quali per la vostra Magnifica Signoria si scriva faccino ragione somaria come fare si de' nele cose pie ale miserabili persone. La quale cosa perchè è iusta, misericordiosa et pia, per gratia singulare a noi proprii essere fatta riputeremo dala vostra excelsa Signoria, ala quale humilmente ci racomandiamo. Parati semper vestre Magnifice dominationis parere mandatis. Datum in terra Montispoli-tiani XXXprimo martii 1438.

Document 16

LIBER REFORMATIONUM, 1437–41,
f. 199r
31 OCTOBER 1439

Secundo. Cum tumulus seu sepultura domini Bartholomey Franciscy Bartholomey completus ac fulcita sit, et orta sit differentia propterea inter magistrum Michelozum . . . de Florentia, ex parte una, et donnum Batistam priorem Parcie, ex parte alia. Ideo pro interesse Comunis viso quod omne residuum hereditatis dicti Francisci seu domini Bartholomey debet per-venire fraternitati et opere plebis huius terre et puellis nubendis, provideatur in predictis et dependentibus ab eisdem ut dictis consiliis placuerit generaliter proponendo.

Document 17

LIBER REFORMATIONUM, 1437–41,
f. 200r
31 OCTOBER 1439

pro sepultura domini Bartholomey francisci

Michelangelus Niccolay aringando consuluit super dicta secunda proposita differentie tumuli domini Bartholomey Franciscy. Quod audita re-latione facta in presenti consilio, modus iste servetur, videlicet. Quod si Magister Andreas . . . et Magister Masius . . ., ambo magistri intagli, qui praticaverunt super extimatione dicte sepul-ture et operis, sunt concordes de extimatione dicte facte sepulture, veniatur in presentia huius consilii. Et si retuleritur esse in concordia exti-matio dicte sepulture et operis per eos facta, valeat et teneat et effectualiter observetur et ulterius non procedatur. Sin autem provideatur et fiat ut consilio opus esse videbitur.

f. 200v

Simili modo dato partito, victum obtentum et deliberatum fuit secundum consilium per dictum Michelangelum super dicta secunda proposita ut supra redditum, per lupinos albos XLIII pro sic redditos, viginti rubeis pro non redditis non obstantibus.

Document 18

COPIALETTERA 3, f. 66v
14 JANUARY 1440

Magnifici et potentes patres et domini nostri singularissimi &c. Ricorre ala magnificentia vostra Il venerabile huomo don baptista priore de la parcia dilectissimo nostro terriero per certa differentia ha con michelozo maestro d'intaglio vostro ciptadino per cagione dal quanti pagamenti fatti per una sepultura di marmo qui fatta con figure intagliate. come da lui particolare informatione haver potrà la magnificentia vostra. Il perche conosciuto lui esser uomo semplice e puro con ardentissima affectione in quelle cose che con ragione e honestà si conprendera per la uostra M.S. poterli prestare favore a la magnificentia vostra lo racomandiamo. Et ciascuno piacere et favore per la M. vostra che a lui si presterà et farà a noi proprii esser prestato e fatto per gratia lo riputeremo. Parati semper vestre M.^{ce} S. parere mandatis. Datum in terra Montispolitianj. die XIIIj. Januarii a nativitate M.CCCC.XXXX°.

Document 19

VISITATIO CIVITATIS, AC DIOCESIS TOTIUS MONTIS POLITIANI FACTA PER ILL^{em} AC R^{dum} D. D. ANGELUM PERUTIUM EPISCOPUM SARSINAT., ff. 17–18

MS OF 1583 IN ARCHIVIO OF THE DUOMO, MONTEPULCIANO.

'Altare sancti Angeli est lateritium cum suo altare portatile, est munitum Palio satis decente non tamen habet candelabra que conveniat et prop.^{ea} ord.^{t} prouidend^m de candelabris, ac de cruce decente.

Ad ipsum Altare habentur duo tituli beneficiati quorum Prior dicitur S.^{tus} Angelus prior cuius Rector R. C. Florentius Belarmenius Abbas, est habet in bonis stabilibus stania sexaginta bene araticie, et unam domum in Ciuitate cum onere celebrandi alternis diebus Domenicis et duobus diebus cuiuslibet hebdomade, et cum Tassa Studij. Alius titulus qui dicitur Sanctus Angelus secundus cuius est Rector D. Julius cinus canonicus in ipsa Ecc.^{a} habet in bonis petiam unam bene araticiam staniorum quatuor ut circa, vineam unam et domum unam et ut dictum fuit habet etiam olivetam unam suos confines, cum onere celebrandi quibuslibet alternis diebus Dominicis et duobus diebus in hebdomada et ambo tituli dicuntur cap.^{le} integre . . .

Et quum Idem R.^{mus} Visitator uidit ad ipsum altare Iconam aliquam non haberi sed loco Icone haberi sepulchrum unum marmoreum cum duabus statuis marmoreis, et aliis quam pluribus figuris in marmore ipso desculptis fabricatum ut apparuit anno mill.^{mo} quatring.^{mo} octuag.^{mo} (*sic*) cum laminis et inscriptione huius tenoris, viz.

Amatori patriae Conseruatori Reipublicae, Bartholomeo / doctissimo apud Martinum Quintum Pontificem Max.^{m} / Consiliorum omnium participi, immature absumpto / posteri dedicauerunt et benemerenti. Et in pedestallo ipsius sepulchri, haec alia est inscriptio, viz. Fidelis affinis, et Compatriota mihi executor fuit / S. Joannes barti.^{ei} anno dni 1438.

Quod ualde indecens esse iudicauit idem R.^{mus} D. Visitator, et propterea ord.^{it} sepulchrum ipsum inde prorsus remoueri, et in eius locum apponi tabulam seu Iconam pulchram cum Imagine eiusdem S.^{ti} cuius sunt tituli dictorum beneficiorum. Quod si fieri non possit sine scandalo ord.^{it} Altare ipsum remoueri, et titulos peremptos ad aliquod aliud ex Altaribus in d.^{a} ecc.^{a} existentibus transferri cum omnibus honoribus, et oneribus, ac iuribus, et actionibus eorumdem.'

Glossary

abbreviator

Officials of the Papal chancery, specially charged with the duty of turning petitions presented to the Pope and granted by him into the form of a minute (*minuta* or *nota*), that is the draft of a Papal rescript (bull or letter).

acheiropitos

Not painted by human hand, applied to certain much venerated images of the Virgin and Child, believed to be of supernatural origin.

arcipresbiterato

The office of *arciprete* (q.v.); also the church and its subordinate district in charge of an *arciprete* (arch-priest), just as the modern English rural deanery is the ecclesiastical district of a rural dean.

arciprete

Arch-priest, a dignity no longer in use in the Anglican church, but still found in the Catholic church, especially in Italy and Spain. In Italy, applied to a priest in charge of one of the subdivisions of a diocese (English deanery), or to the chief dignitary of a chapter, or to the rector of a *chiesa matrice* (mother church).

arcipretura

The office of *arciprete* (arch-priest); also a parish in charge of an *arciprete*.

Arte di Calimala

The Florentine guild of merchants who finished and sold cloth imported from the North, mostly Flanders and France. The guild reached its greatest importance in the thirteenth century, but still enjoyed high standing in the fifteenth.

berretta

A hat, at this date the conical, flat-topped bonnet worn by men of noble and knightly estate and by prelates.

brigata

A group of comrades, used of a set of friends who habitually consort together.

buticularius

Butler, i.e. the household officer in charge of the stock of drink and of its service.

camarlingo (camarlengo)

Treasurer, in an Italian town or city, more or less the equivalent of a modern borough treasurer, i.e. an official who received and accounted for the town revenues. Also applied to the treasurer of a public office, of a monastery, confraternity or other society.

campione

General account-book.

cancelliere

lit. Chancellor, in Italian cities and towns, the official charged with the public correspondence (i.e. a sort of town clerk).

canonicato

In this book the common residence of the canons regular of a church or cathedral. Also a canonry.

cantoria

A balcony for the organ and choir in an Italian church.

Capitani di Parte Guelfa

The heads of the Guelf or Papal party, who in Florence and its *contado* became part of the structure of the civic government in order to ensure the rule of the party. By the fifteenth century their opponents, the Ghibellines, were a thing of the past, but the *capitani* continued to be elected as before.

capostipite

Literally the head of the family stem, in Italian usage the founder of a family, from whose Christian name its surname was often derived.

cappuccio

Hood, at this date attached to the back of the collar of the cloak, so that it could be pulled up to protect the head.

catasto

A general tax on property, first levied in Florence in 1427. It involved a return, to be made by all those liable to the tax, of their property, together with a *stima* (estimate) of its value and an account of any income drawn from it, whether in money or in kind.

Capitani of the Arti

The heads of the Florentine guilds (*arti*).

capomaestro della fabbrica

Head of the works on a building project.

cedula

A document bearing the record of a monetary transaction, forming a written obligation, but drawn up without the assistance of a notary.

commenda

A system whereby an ecclesiastical benefice or a church or monastery was given (*commended*) to a non-resident holder.

consoli di mare

The magistrates in charge of maritime trade and all disputes over sea-traffic.

contadino

Inhabitant of the *contado* (q.v.), therefore a peasant.

contado

lit. County, in practice the territory outside the walls of an Italian city under the control of that city.

contrada

A street.

corrector

Officials of the Papal chancery, whose duty was to examine the minute prepared by the *abbreviatores* (q.v.). After the minute had been engrossed on parchment by the *scriptores* (q.v.), the *corrector* examined the *grossa* to see if it was correctly made out and in agreement with the original Papal decision. It was then his duty to divide the engrossed letters into two categories, those which were read before the Pope once more before delivery, and those which were read before the *auditores litterarum contradictarum*.

denaro picciolo

The smallest of Florentine coins; in Florentine accounting equivalent to a twelfth of a *soldo* (q.v.), and to 1/240 of a *lira picciola* (q.v.).

depositario

A treasurer, here a banker accredited to be a treasurer of the Papal Curia.

dispensator

Household officer in charge of the distribution of provisions.

Dodici Buonuomini

lit. Twelve good men and true. Elected magistrates, first appointed in 1321.

donzello

lit. A youth, here a sergeant-at-arms.

emptor

Household officer in charge of purchases for the household.

fermaglio

Brooch; in the context of ecclesiastical costume, a morse. Used to clasp together two sides of a garment.

fiorino

Florin, a Florentine coin and one of the most popular currencies of the Middle Ages. So called from the gold coin first minted in 1252 by the Republic of Florence. The silver coin was worth a twentieth part of the gold florin.

gabella

A tax levied at town-gates on merchandise and other dutiable property brought in or brought out; in Florence also a tax on contracts.

giuspatronato

The right of patronage or presentation to an ecclesiastical benefice, church or *opera pia* (e.g. a hospital), acquired in virtue of having founded and endowed it.

Gonfaloniere

lit. Standard-bearer. The title was originally given to the man who had the right to carry the banners of the Comune or of a section of the Comune in popular assemblies or military expeditions. In Florence, the *Gonfaloniere di giustizia* was the supreme magistrate of the city. The title of Gonfaloniere was also used in other Tuscan cities for the supreme magistrate.

invitatore

A man deputed to issue invitations to a solemn occasion. In medieval Tuscany the name given to a messenger sent round by the Comune, or by a guild or confraternity, to invite the persons named by a dead man's family, friends or executors to attend his funeral.

lira piccola

Lire piccole (*lit.* small pounds) were imaginary coins, used in accounting. The *lira piccola* was equivalent to 20 *soldi piccoli* (q.v.) or 240 *denari piccoli* (q.v.).

lire cortonesi

Lire minted at Cortona.

maggiordomo

The governor of the household, responsible to its master for its general organisation and supervision.

mastro-libro

More usually *libro maestro*, ledger.

metadella

Glossed by Florio-Torriano in 1659 as 'a certain little measure about a wine-pinte'.

notarius camparie del comune

In Montepulciano, a judge with special jurisdiction over rural matters.

oncia

The twelfth part of a lira (pound). Used in the Middle Ages as a weight for gold and silver coins and also as the name of a gold coin that circulated in the Kingdom of Naples.

opera

lit. Board of works. The terms used to describe a board of citizens appointed to oversee the maintenance and improvement of buildings and churches where this was considered a civic or guild responsibility.

operaio

Member of a board of works.

oratore

In fifteenth-century Italian usage, an envoy, or man charged with a public mission.

Ordo Romanus

A ritual book containing instructions for the ceremonial to be observed in the various liturgical functions of the Roman Curia. Quite a number of varying age have come down to us from the Middle Ages: fifteen were first collected and published by Mabillon in 1689.

palazuolo

lit. Big palace, here simply a large cottage.

panetarius

The household official in charge of its bread.

parlamento

In Tuscany, a general assembly of the people.

peperino

Peperin, a volcanic tufa found in the Alban hills near Rome.

pergamo

Pulpit.

piazza

See *seggio.*

pietra serena

A grey stone, found at Fiesole and Settignano.

pievano

Parish priest.

pieve

The parish church, the principal church of a town or village, as opposed to churches which are not parish churches and may be subordinate to the *pieve.*

platea

See *seggio.*

plebatus

The parish of a *pieve.*

Podestà

A magistrate appointed from outside an Italian city, to do justice and carry out other administrative functions within it, usually for the term of a year. He was a sort of combination of mayor, judge and sheriff.

portata al catasto

A tax-return, made to the Florentine officials who had to impose the *catasto* (q.v.). Generally contains invaluable details about the family and occupation of the returner, as well as about his property.

prestanza

lit. Loan; a polite name for a forced public loan, really a levy of tax.

priorato

Priory.

proposto

lit. Provost. As an Italian ecclesiastical dignitary, the head of a collegiate church.

provveditore

An official deputed to oversee and administer certain sorts of public business.

quaderno di cassa

Cash-book.

scriptor

Officials of the Papal chancery, whose duty was to engross on parchment according to the rules of the chancery the minutes prepared by the *abbreviatores*. Their full title was *scriptores litterarum apostolicarum*: they were also known as *grossatores*.

seggio (plural seggi)

A *seggio* was both a ward of the city of Naples and the meeting-place (*lit. seggio*, seat) where the nobles of the ward met together to transact its business. Hence, it can also mean the council of the nobles. Also known as *sedile* (*lit.* seat), *platea* (*lit.* square), *piazza* (square), and *tocco*.

Sei della Mercatanzia

A Florentine tribunal appointed by the twelve major guilds of the city to settle disputes between Florentine merchants and between Florentine and non-Florentine merchants.

Signoria

lit. Lordship. The term usually applied to the ruling magistrates of Florence.

soldo piccolo

An imaginary coin, used in accounting: traditionally the twentieth of a *lira*.

sotto scrivano

Under-clerk.

Spedalingo

Head of a hospital.

staio (pl. staia)

A measure equivalent to a bushel: used also as a measure of land.

stima

Evaluation, appraisal of the money-value of goods or of a work of art.

studium generale

University.

tabarro

A long, loose cloak with a collar.

targhetta

A small shield.

terziere

lit. A third part, in Siena and Montepulciano indicating a ward of the city.

tocco

See *seggio*.

travertino

Travertine, a stone found near Rome and in Tuscany.

Ufficiali dei Pupilli

A Florentine official body with responsibility for the custody of wards.

uomini da bene

Men of good standing.

xenodochium

Monastery, hospital.

The Popes of The Great Schism

Obedience of Avignon From September 1378	**Obedience of Rome**	**Obedience of The Council of Pisa**

CLEMENT VII
(Robert of Geneva)
Elected 20 September 1378
d. 16 September 1394

BENEDICT XIII
(Pedro de Luna of Aragon)
Elected 28 September 1394
d. 23 May 1423

URBAN VI
(Bartolommeo Prignano of Naples)
Elected 8 April 1378
d. 15 October 1389

BONIFACE IX
(Pietro Tomacelli of Naples)
Elected 2 November 1389
d. 1 October 1404

INNOCENT VII
(Cosimo Migliorati of Sulmona)
Elected 17 October 1404
d. 6 November 1406

GREGORY XII
(Angelo Correr of Venice)
Elected 30 November 1406
d. 4 July 1415

ALEXANDER V
(Pietro Philargo of Crete)
Elected 26 June 1409
d. 3 May 1410

JOHN XXIII
(Baldassare Cossa of Naples)
Elected 17 May 1410
d. 22 December 1419

MARTIN V
(Odo Colonna of Rome)
Elected 11 November 1417
d. 20 February 1431

Chronology of Donatello

This is designed to provide a background to the works discussed in the present book: all conjectural dates are omitted. I wish to acknowledge a debt to the very useful PROSPETTO CRONOLOGICO *drawn up by Dr. Luigi Grassi for his* TUTTA LA SCULTURA DI DONATELLO, *Milan, 1963, pp. 48–56; the present chronology incorporates corrections and additions. Perhaps attention may be specially drawn to the unpublished fifteenth-century document concerning Donatello's tomb included at the end. All dates are given modern style.*

1386	Donato di Niccolò di Betto Bardi is born in Florence, the son of Niccolò di Bardo, a wool-carder and his wife Orsa. As was not unusual in the fifteenth century, Donatello varied in his statements of his age; 1386 is generally accepted as his birth date, which corresponds to his age as given in two of his tax-returns (the *portate al catasto* of 1427 and 1433), but the year 1382 is implied by the age stated in his last tax-return of 1457. Vasari says that he was born in 1383
1403, May 1407	Donatello is mentioned as working in the shop of Lorenzo Ghiberti and of Cione di Ser Buonaccorso, Donatello's godfather
1406, 23 November–1408, February	Records of payments for small marble figures of prophets to be set on the Porta della Mandorla of the Duomo of Florence
1408, 20 February	Donatello is comissioned to carve a figure of *David* to be set on the tribune of the Duomo (transferred in 1416 to Palazzo Vecchio)
1408, 19 December	Donatello is commissioned to carve a marble statue of *St. John the Evangelist* for the façade of the Duomo
1409, 13 June	A record of a payment still due for the figure of a prophet
1411, 3 April	The *Arte de' Linaiuoli* commission a figure of *San Marco* from Donatello for one of the niches on Or San Michele
1412	Donatello, described as *'orafo e scarpellatore'* is enrolled in the Compagnia di San Luca, the artist's confraternity of Florence
1412, 12 August	A note of payment due from the Opera del Duomo for the *David* and for the *St. John the Evangelist*

1415, 9 October	Donatello and Brunelleschi are paid for a marble statue, draped in gilt lead, made as a model for the large figures to be set on the tribune of the Duomo
1415, 5 December	The *Opera del Duomo* commission two statues of white marble from Donatello for the Campanile
1417, February	The *Opera del Duomo* sell the Arte de' Corazzai marble for the base of Donatello's statue of *St. George* on Or San Michele
1418, 11 March	The *Opera del Duomo* make a payment to Donatello for the two figures for the Campanile
1418, 28 June–23 December	The *Opera del Duomo* make payments to Donatello for two marble figures
1419, 11 October	The *Opera del Duomo* make an advance to Donatello for a marble figure for the Campanile
1419, 29 December	Donatello, Brunelleschi and Nanni di Banco are paid 45 florins for a model of the cupola of the Duomo
1420, 9 January and 21 February	Donatello is paid by the *Opera del Duomo* for the *Marzocco*, or figure of the Florentine lion
1421, 10 March	The *Opera del Duomo* commission the group of the *Sacrifice of Isaac* from Donatello and Nanni di Banco
1421, 6 November	The *Opera* completes its payments for the *Sacrifice of Isaac*
c. 1421–c. 1428	Donatello at first by himself, later in partnership with Michelozzo, carves the tomb of Baldassare Cossa (Pope John XXIII) in the Baptistery of Florence
1422, 13 May	Donatello is paid for the *Head of a prophet* and the *Head of a Sibyl*, to be set in Nanni di Banco's relief above the Porta della Mandorla
1423, 10 February	The *Soprastanti alla Fabbrica* (Board of Works) of the cathedral of Orvieto take steps to commission a gilt copper figure of *St. John the Baptist* from Donatello, to be set on their font
1423, 9 March	Payment of 9 florins for a marble figure in progress for the Campanile
1423, 29 April	Donatello receives wax to make a model for the Orvieto *Baptist* (see above)
1423, 14 and 19 May	The *Parte Guelfa* of Florence authorises a payment to Donatello so that he may complete the figure of *San Lodovico*, to be set in a niche on Or San Michele

1423, May	Donatello receives a first payment on account from the *Opera del Duomo* of Siena for the bronze relief of the *Banquet of Herod* for the Baptismal Font
1425, March	The *Banquet of Herod* has not been finished on time, and the *Opera del Duomo* of Siena decide to demand the return of the money advanced for it.
1425, 16 May	Donatello is owed 16 florins in part payment for a statue for the Campanile of the Duomo in Florence
1426, 18 February	A valuation is made by Filippo Lippi, Niccolò Spinelli and Andrea di Onofrio of a figure carved by Donatello for the Duomo
1426, 18 March	Donatello is paid for a figure executed for the Duomo
1426, 16 April–12 August	Payments are made to Donatello by the Medici bank
c. 1426–*c.* 1428	Donatello and Michelozzo carve the tomb of Cardinal Rainaldo Brancaccio in Sant'Angelo a Nido, Naples. The tomb is carved in Pisa, where Donatello's presence is documented in July and December 1426
1427, 11 February	A payment is made to Donatello for a statue for the Duomo
1427, 13 April	By this date the *Banquet of Herod* has reached Siena
1427, 9 May	Donatello and Michelozzo ask for the speedy payment of 50 florins promised them by the Opera del Duomo of Siena
1427, 8 October	Final payment for the *Banquet of Herod*
1428, 14 July–1438, 17 September	Donatello and Michelozzo carve the Prato pulpit
1428, 25 September; 1429, 1 April	Payments for the gilt bronze figures of *Faith* and *Hope* intended for the Baptismal Font of Siena
1429, 16 April	The *Opera del Duomo* of Siena record a payment for wax furnished to Donatello to make models for the three nude bronze child angels set on the Baptismal Font
1429, 18 April	A note of the payments already made by the *Opera del Duomo* of Siena for bronze figures of *Faith* and *Hope*
1429, 22 April	Donatello is making a small tabernacle door for the Baptismal Font of Siena
1430, 23 September	Donatello is in Rome
1432, 28 or 29 July	Death in Rome of Giovanni Crivelli, archdeacon of Aquileja, Papal *scriptor* and *abbreviator*. Donatello goes to Rome to make a valuation of the bronze tomb of Pope Martin V, in

	St. John Lateran, and while there carves Crivelli's tombslab, now in Santa Maria in Aracoeli
1433, early months	Donatello is still in Rome, and in all probability carves the *Tabernacolo del Sacramento* for St. Peter's (now in the Cappella dei Beneficiati)
1433, 1 April	Pagno di Lapo is sent to Rome to bring back Donatello to work on the Prato Pulpit
1433, 31 May	Donatello is back in Florence
1433, 10 July	Donatello is commissioned by the Opera del Duomo to carve a *Cantoria* for the Duomo of Florence
1434, 31 January	Donatello receives a payment for a statue of *Habakkuk*
1434, 12 April	Donatello enters a design for the competition for a *Coronation of the Virgin* to be executed in stained glass for a window in the drum of Brunelleschi's dome
1434, 27 July	Donatello and Luca della Robbia are commissioned to make a terracotta head as a ceiling boss for Brunelleschi's dome
1434, 12 August	Donatello acquires a large block of marble for a tomb
1434, 4 October	Donatello is paid for his design for the stained glass window of the dome
1435, 15 June	A payment on account for the *Habakkuk*
1436, 11 January	The *Habakkuk*, now finished, has been valued at 90 florins
1437, 14 February to 6 April	Donatello is commissioned to make the bronze doors for the two sacristies of the Duomo of Florence: the commission was later transferred to Luca della Robbia on Donatello's failure to make them
1437	Ciriaco of Ancona visits Donatello in his workshop
1438, 20 June	The *Cantoria* is by now almost finished
1439, 12 October	Donatello is given bronze with which to cast a head to be set on the lower part of the *Cantoria* to match the bronze head already there
1440, 12 January and 5 February	The *Cantoria* is complete and Donatello receives a payment on account
1443	Donatello leaves Florence and goes to Padua, where he will remain until 1454 or 1455

1444, 24 January	He has already been commissioned by the Fabbricieri of the Santo to make a *Crucifix* in bronze
1444, 19 June	A record that Donatello has received 21 lb. of white wax for the *Crucifix*
1445, July	The *Crucifix* is still not ready
1446, 13 April	A gift by Francesco Tergola to the *Opera* of the Santo of 1500 lire to pay for a new altarpiece for the high altar is accepted, and the work is commissioned from Donatello
1447, 11 February	Donatello and his assistants receive a payment for the altarpiece and wax to make models for the heads of the figures in it
1447, 4 April	Payment for copper supplied to Donatello for casting figures for the altarpiece
1447, 29 April	Donatello is commissioned by the *Massari dell'Arca* to execute ten bronze reliefs of angels and four bronze reliefs of the symbols of the Evangelists. The angels had in fact already been cast and were to be chased and prepared for gilding
1447, 10 May	A payment to Andrea delle Caldiere for casting the ten angels, two of the symbols of the Evangelists and one of the reliefs of the miracles of St. Anthony of Padua
1447, 16 May	Payments for the stone base of the Gattamelata monument
1447, May–June	Payments for casting parts of the Gattamelata monument and for removing it from Donatello's workshop
1447, 19 June	Payment to Andrea dal Mayo for casting two reliefs of the miracles of St. Anthony, two reliefs of the Evangelists and a figure of St. Louis of Toulouse
1447, 22 June	Donatello's assistants have worked on two angels and one of the symbols of the Evangelists
1447, 23 June	Donatello undertakes to complete the four reliefs of the miracles of St. Anthony and two figures of St. Francis of Assisi and St. Louis of Toulouse within eight months. Of the reliefs three had in fact been cast, but had not yet been chased and finished, while one had not yet been modelled; of the two saints, wax models only had been made
1447, 15 November	Payment for the casting of the fourth relief of the miracles of St. Anthony
1448, 7 February, March–May	Payments for casting the figures of the altar

325

1448, 23 April	Payment to Donatello for eight columns to make a temporary altar on 13 June 1448, the festival of St. Anthony, to show the proposed design of the altarpiece to strangers
1448, 17–18 May	The statue of the Virgin for the altarpiece has been modelled and a mould prepared, but it has not yet been cast
1448, 25 May	The Virgin has been cast and has now been brought into the church
1448, 5 June	A note of money due for the seven bronze figures of the Virgin and saints
1448, 13 June	On the temporary altar, are set up eight columns, the figures of the Virgin and saints, two reliefs of angels, the relief of the *Pietà*, a relief in stone of the *Deposition*, a relief in stone of God the Father, and four other reliefs in stone
1448, 26 June	Four of the reliefs of angels have been chased: Donatello is paid for these and receives a payment for casting a fifth (compare 1447, 29 April)
1448, 1 July	A note of money due for the four bronze reliefs of the miracles of St. Anthony, which are still unfinished, exclusive of silvering and gilding
1448, 13 September– 1449, 6 May	Payments for gold and silver acquired by Donatello for silvering and gilding the bronze figures and reliefs of the altarpiece
1449, 7–29 January	Niccolò Pizzolo is paid for painting the cross for Donatello's *Crucifix*, and a woman is paid for gilding the cross
1449, 29 January	Donatello is paid for silvering and gilding of the four *Miracles* of St. Anthony
1449, 12 February	Payment to a Florentine mason for eight marble columns, four of them square, the other four round and fluted, executed for the high altar of the Santo
1449, 26 April	A note of money due to Donatello for five stone reliefs, with figures, *The Entombment*
1449, 23–26 June	Donatello is paid for a relief in stone of God the Father above the 'cupola' of the altar, also for arranging for the making of a marble antependium, for gilding two of the reliefs of angels and for gilding the *Pietà*
1450, 13 June	The Santo altar is solemnly unveiled in Padua
1450, May	Donatello sends to Mantua a number of figures, subject reliefs, and architectural columns

1450–51	Donatello is in Mantua, where Marchese Lodovico has commissioned him to make a tomb for the body of St. Anselm. This was never executed
1451, 9 January	Record of payment of 10 ducats due to Donatello from the Bishop of Ferrara
1451, 10 March	Donatello goes to Modena, where he agrees with the Savi del Comune to make an equestrian statue in gilt bronze of Borso d'Este, Marchese of Ferrara. Soon afterwards he leaves Modena without undertaking the work, which is never executed in spite of a renewed promise by Donatello made in Padua in February
1454, April	Donatello is apparently still in Padua, but he dislikes the Paduans and has no wish to die there
1455, April	Donatello, now back in Florence, and Michelozzo ask the *Operai* of Prato to settle their outstanding account
1456, 24 March	Donatello, still in Florence, appoints an agent to collect the money still owing to him for the altar of the Santo in Padua
1456, 27 August	Donatello has been treated by the Florentine physician Giovanni Chellini to whom he presents a bronze relief of the Virgin in gratitude for his cure
1457	Donatello, in Florence, makes a bronze figure of *St. John the Baptist*, cast in three pieces, for the Duomo of Siena
1457, 17 October–10 December	Donatello has taken up residence in Siena, where some of the citizens urge the Balia to find work for him. He is commissioned to make bronze doors for the Duomo, but gets no further than making wax models
1458	Donatello goes with Urbano da Cortona to the alabaster quarries at Velorcia
1458, 8 July	The *Opera del Duomo* of Siena commission a marble figure of *San Bernardino*, but it is never carved
1461, 6 March	Donatello is still in Siena
1465, 15 June	This date is engraved on the bronze relief of the *Martyrdom of San Lorenzo*, set in the south pulpit of San Lorenzo, in Florence. The north and south pulpits of San Lorenzo, commissioned by the Medici, are Donatello's last major works
1466, 13 December	Donatello dies in a house in the Via del Cocomero, Florence. Since the location of his tomb is generally regarded as untraced (cf. H. W. Janson, in *Dizionario biografico degli italiani*, vi, 1964, p. 294) it may be of interest to publish here the relevant extracts from the original *Repertorio delle*

327

Sepolture, che si ritrouano in S. Lorenzo fatte al tempo di Cosimo a Medicis Pater Patrie fatto da Prete Betti Priore (Ms. Magl. XXVI.˙ 171 in Biblioteca Nazionale, Florence). The book runs from 1463 to at least 1483

f. 63ᵛ

L'Anno 1463
+ xhs: MCCCCLXIII

Qui di sotto chome segue faro richordo et schrittura io prete piero priore di Sᵗᵒ Lorenzo dell ordine et forma della sepulture nuoue ha fatto cosmo di medici et gli altri di sotto la chiesa et da chi allogheremo dette sepulture et in che luogo et parte accio si possino ritrouare et prima.

Cominciando dalla Cappella maggiore et quella da lato della mano dextra in uerso la sagrestia et di poi dalla mano sinistra di uerso borgo la noce: et delle teste della Croce et dallato di dette cioè dalli operai et di Luca di marcho, et seguendo di poi la piè gli scaglioni di dette capelle le sepolture della Croce di dᵃ Chiesa, che di sotto per rispetto de pilastri cinque che sostengono le volte fanno dua naue, o vero anditi, ne quali anditi fra scaglione et scaglioni di cappelle sono 4 filari di sepolture nel piano di detta nave andando per lo lungo donde si entra di sotto la cappella de medici allato alla sagrestia per la scala del Chiostro in detto Cimitero et sepolture e seguendo infino alla testa et cappella della Croce di detta nave di uerso borgo la noce, che el primo filare del pie la cappella maggiore, e l'altre dallato per ire sino ad hora murate fanno sepolture XXVI: dalla sagrestia in fino alla Cappella della stufa cioè Sepolture 26.

Secondo filare allato al predetto che uiene a essere trà pilastri, che sostengono le uolte, exetto tre sepolture mozze che sono a piè di trè pilastri di verso le cappelle et trà detto filare il filare di sopra nominato in tutto per lo lungo andando quelle che sono fatte infino a qui fanno numero 19.

Medici – 3 – Alla casa et discendenti di Giovanni daverardo de medici una sepultura darca marmorea in detta sagrestia et dua altre sepolture di marmo sotto detta archa ouero dallato coperte con uno desco grande di marmo et in mezo di sopra un tondo di porfido dove si pongono e paramenti della chiesa.

Alla capella della croce allato alla sagrestia et coniunta a detta, che è di giovanni di averardo de medici la qual muro insieme con detta sagrestia et de suoi non ue per insino al di doggi sepultura nessuna per che ue l'entrata di sotto et la scala che mette per il chiostro indetto cimitero et a dette sepulture.

f. 67ᵛ   . . . . . .

Seguita il secondo filare della + (croce): prima A Maestro Donato (in another hand *als Donatello* to fill a blank) nobilissimo sculptore per commessione Del mag.ᶜᵒ piero di cosimo de medici la pᵐᵃ del secondo filare di detter croce allato al predetto filare tra pilastro e pilastro che sostengono le volte in cominciando apiè lo scaglione di sotto la capella allate alla sagrestia de medici chentra nel cimitero che insino a hora sono sepulture finite al quaderno scritta 141 nᵒ 29.

                                                        . . . . . .

[17] Al magnifico et excellente cosmo di Gⁿⁱ daverardo de medici padre della patria nel terzo pilastro che sostiene le uolte di riscontro all altare magiore fornito di sotto e di sopra tutto di marmo porfidi et altre pietre di pregio una magnifica sepultura fuori & di sopra al piano delle sepulture di sotto et nescie (n'esce) col piano di sopra nel pavimento della chiesa dinanzi allaltare maggiore'.

Chronology of Michelozzo

As with that of Donatello, this is designed to provide a background to the works discussed in the book: all conjectural dates are omitted. I wish to acknowledge my obligations to Fabriczy's chronology, preceding his biographical and documentary study of the artist (cited as Fabriczy here) and to Professor Harriet Caplow's published thesis, MICHELOZZO, New York & London, 1977, which produces new documentary evidence, especially for the events of Michelozzo's later life.
All dates are given modern style.

1396	Birth of Michelozzo, son of Bartolommeo di Gherardo detto Borgognone and his wife Antonia di Leonardo Porcellini
1410, 28 May	First record of Michelozzo as engraver to the Zecca (mint) of Florence
1420–22	Michelozzo assists Ghiberti to make the bronze statue of San Matteo for the *Arte del Cambio* on Or San Michele, Florence, and on the North doors of the Baptistery
1425, 2 January	Michelozzo is working with Ghiberti on the second (East) doors of the Baptistery
c. 1425–26	Michelozzo and Donatello enter into partnership
1427, 9 May	A letter from Donatello and Michelozzo jointly to the *Operaio* of the Duomo of Siena, requesting payment for the bronze relief of the *Banquet of Herod,* made by Donatello for the Baptismal Font
1428, August	Michelozzo is with Donatello in Pisa
c. 1426–27	The Aragazzi tomb is commissioned from Donatello and Michelozzo
1430, 20 March to 14 June	Michelozzo is at the Florentine camp before Lucca
1430, 28 December	Michelozzo is in Padua
1432, summer	Michelozzo goes with Donatello to Rome
1432, 28 December	Michelozzo is in Montepulciano
1433, April	Michelozzo is back in Florence
1436	Work on the Aragazzi tomb halts for want of money

1437, 4 April to 1442	Michelozzo again assists Ghiberti in making the second set of bronze doors for the Baptistery of Florence
1437	The cloister of San Marco begun, to a design by Michelozzo
1438	Completion of the Aragazzi tomb
1439–41	Michelozzo rebuilds the choir of San Marco, whose *giuspatronato* had been acquired by Cosimo de' Medici in 1438
1440, 16 October	The Comune of Montepulciano officially invite Michelozzo to submit a design for their new Palazzo
1441, January or February	Michelozzo marries Francesca, daughter of Piero di Ambrogio (a tanner), who is aged about eighteen
7 February	Notarial contracts are made concerning the dowry of Michelozzo's wife Francesca
1441, late December or early January 1442	Birth of Michelozzo's eldest son, Bartolommeo
1442, September to December	Birth of Piero, Michelozzo's second son
1442, 28 August	In his *portata al catasto* of this date, Michelozzo declares that he has had no work for two years
1443, 10 October	Michelozzo acquires a *vigna* at San Donnino a Brozzi
1444	Birth of Michelozzo's daughter, Antonia
1444	Palazzo Medici in Via Larga begun to Michelozzo's design
1444, 5 (10) October	Michelozzo first recorded as the *capomaestro* of the Chiesa dell' Annunziata (Santa Maria dei Servi), Florence
1444, 30 December	Michelozzo and his partners Maso di Bartolommeo and Giovanni di Bartolommeo are paid for two bronze handles made for the cupboards of the sacristy of the Duomo
1445, 28 February	Michelozzo and his partners are paid for two copper balls made for the lamps of the high altar of the Duomo
1446, 28 February	Michelozzo, Luca della Robbia and Maso di Bartolommeo enter into a contract with the *Opera del Duomo* to make the bronze doors for the north sacristy of the Duomo, Donatello having failed to honour his contract
1446, 11 August	Michelozzo is appointed to complete the building of Brunelleschi's dome on the death of Brunelleschi
1446, 29 November	The Florentine *Compagnia de' Magi* take measures to hold an especially splendid festival in honour of the Magi next

	Epiphany; Michelozzo is listed as one of the ten members of the commission appointed by the Compagnia for this purpose
1446, 22 December	Michelozzo and his partners are paid for bronze steps they have made by the *Opera del Duomo*
c. 1447	Michelozzo submits a scheme to the Florentine *Signoria* for draining the Palude di Castiglione, near Grosseto
1447, 23 February	The *Parte Guelfa* decide to complete the new sacristy of the Chiesa dell' Annunziata, whose reconstruction has been begun to the design of Michelozzo
28 February	Michelozzo is commissioned by the *Opera del Duomo* to make a bronze grating for the new altar of the chapel of St. Stephen
1447, December	Birth of Michelozzo's third son, Niccolò
1448, 18 May	Michelozzo is commissioned by the *Opera del Duomo* to undertake certain works in connection with the walls of Castellina di Greve, in Chianti
1448, 11 October	The *Signoria* of Florence ask the *Operai del Duomo* to hand over to Michelozzo a bell then hanging in the campanile so that it can be used in the new clock at present being made for the Palazzo della Signoria
1450, 23 July	Michelozzo and his partner the goldsmith Bartolommeo di Frussino are paid a florin for a bell they are making for the nuns of San Giovanni de' Cavalieri
1450, 7 August	Michelozzo paid for chasing a figure of the Virgin for a cross
1450, 29 September	Michelozzo returns from Carrara, where he had been to see the quarrying of marble for Brunelleschi's dome
1450, 23 December	Michelozzo and two stonemasons are again sent to Carrara to obtain a large piece of marble for the pilasters of the dome
1451, December	Michelozzo ceases as building-master of Brunelleschi's dome
1452, 3 June	Michelozzo commissioned to make the Baptistery's silver altar
1453	Birth of Michelozzo's daughter Marietta, who seems to have died before 1469
1454 or 1455	Birth of Michelozzo's son Bernardo
1455, 13 February	Michelozzo paid for valuing work in the Chiesa dell' Annunziata
1455, 26 April	Michelozzo is mentioned as general *capomaestro* for all the works of the Florentine Servites, who had the church and convent of the Chiesa dell' Annunziata

1457	In his *portata* Michelozzo again declares that he has no work
1457	Birth of Michelozzo's youngest son Leonardo
1459	Birth of Elisabetta, Michelozzo's youngest daughter
1460	Serves as one of the *capomaestri* of the *Ufficiali della Torre* of Florence
1461, May	Michelozzo is in Ragusa, where he is employed by the Senate to improve the fortifications of the city
1464, 9 February	The Comune of Ragusa decides to rebuild the Palazzo del Rettore after it had been damaged by an explosion and receive a proposal that they should call Michelozzo before them and abide by his advice before proceeding further
1464, 27 April	Two members of the *Consiglio Minore* to instruct Michelozzo
1464, 5 May	A proposal to submit Michelozzo's design for the palace to the Council. His scheme is rejected and Giorgio da Sebenico is employed instead
16 May	Two of the Giustiniani, Lords of Chios, make a contract at Ragusa with Michelozzo for him to go to Chios for at least six months, leaving within the next six or eight days, to serve there in his profession of architect and engineer
End of May	Michelozzo departs for Chios, where he remains until 1467, and is reduced to desperate financial straits
1465	Michelozzo's name is recorded from this year until 1471 in *Libro dello Specchio* of the *Arte di Pietra e Legname*, with a note of what he is expected to contribute to the *Arte*
1467, 29 April	Michelozzo and his son Niccolò leave Chios for Constantinople
Summer	While returning from Constantinople to Italy, the ship from Ancona in which Michelozzo and his son Niccolò are travelling is captured by the Venetians
1468, 10 January	Michelozzo and his son Niccolò are in Venice
1468	Michelozzo's daughter Antonia marries Agostino di Gugliadore
1469	His *portata al catasto* of this year merely declares old debts he does not expect to recover, but there is a possibility that it was returned in his absence
1470, October	Michelozzo is in poor health
1471, 22 December	The *Arte dei Maestri di Pietra e Legname* record that Michelozzo has been absent from Florence for some time
1472, 7 October	Michelozzo is buried in his family tomb in San Marco

ILLUSTRATIONS

(i) Head of Baldassare Cossa by Donatello
from the Cossa Tomb in the Baptistery in Florence

(ii) Head of Cardinal Brancaccio by Donatello
from the Brancaccio Tomb in S. Angelo a Nido in Naples

(iii) Head of Bartolommeo Aragazzi by Michelozzo
from the Aragazzi Tomb in the Duomo of Montepulciano

The Cossa Tomb ·
The Brancaccio Tomb ·
The Aragazzi Tomb and
Other Michelozzo Sculptures

1. Upper part of the Tomb of Baldassare Cossa. Florence, Baptistery. Donatello and Michelozzo

2. Tomb of Baldassare Cossa.
Florence, Baptistery. Donatello and Michelozzo

3. Cossa Tomb. Pylon, with Virtues 'Faith', 'Hope' and 'Charity'. Workshop of Donatello

4. Cossa Tomb. Plinth and base. Workshop of Donatello

5. Cossa Tomb. Detail of pylon, showing 'Charity'. Workshop of Donatello

6–7. Cossa Tomb. Detail of pylon, showing 'Faith' and 'Hope'. Workshop of Donatello

8. Cossa Tomb. Detail of 'Faith'. Workshop of Donatello

9. Cossa Tomb. Detail of 'Hope'. Workshop of Donatello

10. Cossa Tomb. Head of 'Faith', profile. Workshop of Donatello

11. Cossa Tomb. Head of 'Charity'. Workshop of Donatello

12. Cossa Tomb. Effigy and bier. Effigy by Donatello;
bier by workshop of Donatello

IOANĒSQVŌDAMPAPA
XXIIĬOBIITFLORENTIEA
ŇODŇIMCCCCXVIIIIXI
KALENDASIANVARII

13. Cossa Tomb. Epitaph of Baldassare Cossa

14-15. Cossa Tomb. Angels holding epitaph. *Above:* Donatello with assistant; *below:* Donatello (?)

16. Cossa Tomb. Detail of effigy seen from above. Donatello

17. Cossa Tomb. Virgin and Child in lunette. Michelozzo

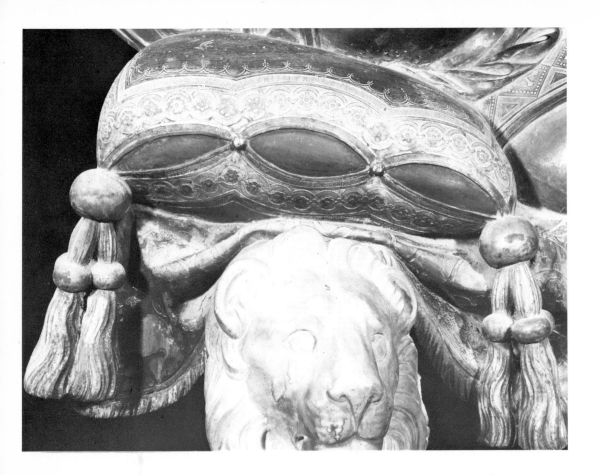

18-19. Cossa Tomb. Detail of bier, pillow and console supporting bier.

20. Cossa Tomb. Detail of Virgin and Child. Michelozzo

21. Tomb of Cardinal Rainaldo Brancaccio. Naples, S. Angelo a Nido.
Donatello and Michelozzo. Old view showing Cardinal's hat suspended from tie rod

22. Tomb of Cardinal Rainaldo Brancaccio. Naples, S. Angelo a Nido.
Donatello and Michelozzo. (Recent view)

23. Brancaccio Tomb. Upper part. Christ in Glory

24. Brancaccio Tomb. Virgin and Child with St. John the Baptist
and St. Michael the Archangel. Workshop of Donatello

25–26. Brancaccio Tomb. Upper part. Putti. Donatello

27. Brancaccio Tomb.
Left spandrel of arch over effigy

28. Brancaccio Tomb.
Capital on left under canopy

29. Brancaccio Tomb. Detail of Virgin and Child. Workshop of Donatello

30. Brancaccio Tomb. Detail of effigy. Donatello

31. Brancaccio Tomb. Upper part. Putto on right. Donatello

32. Brancaccio Tomb. Central section

33. Brancaccio Tomb. Relief panel, 'Assumption of the Virgin'. Donatello

34. Brancaccio Tomb. Central section. Angel on right. Donatello and assistants

35. Brancaccio Tomb. Head of Angel on left. Donatello and assistants

36. Brancaccio Tomb. Head of Angel on right. Donatello and assistants

37. Brancaccio Tomb. Detail of relief panel,
'Assumption of the Virgin'. Donatello

38. Brancaccio Tomb. Detail of relief panel,
'Assumption of the Virgin'. Donatello

39-40. Brancaccio Tomb. Central Caryatid Virtue. Workshop of Donatello

41-42. Brancaccio Tomb. Caryatid Virtues on left and right. Workshop of Donatello

43. Brancaccio Tomb. Head of Caryatid Virtue on left. Workshop of Donatello

44. Brancaccio Tomb. Head of Central Caryatid Virtue. Workshop of Donatello

45. Brancaccio Tomb. Head of Caryatid Virtue on right. Workshop of Donatello

46. Tomb of Bartolommeo Aragazzi. Montepulciano, Duomo. Effigy of Bartolommeo Aragazzi.
Now set on inner side of entrance wall of the Duomo. Michelozzo

47. Aragazzi Tomb. Detail of base.
Now set on the high altar of the Duomo. Workshop of Michelozzo

48. Putto. Detail of 47

49–50. Aragazzi Tomb. Aragazzi welcomed into Paradise by
his Mother and other members of his family; the Virgin blessing Aragazzi in Paradise.
Relief panels now set on two piers of the nave of the Duomo. Michelozzo

51. Aragazzi and his Mother. Detail of 49

52. Two youths. Detail of 49

53. Aragazzi's Mother and three Brothers. Detail of 50

54. Virgin and Child. Detail of 50

55. Virgin and Child. Detail of terracotta relief from façade of
Sant'Agostino, Montepulciano. Michelozzo

56. Aragazzi Tomb. Adoring Angel.
Now in the Victoria and Albert Museum, London. Michelozzo

57. Aragazzi Tomb. Adoring Angel.
Now in the Victoria and Albert Museum, London. Michelozzo

58 (*below*). Aragazzi Tomb. Head of Angel. Detail of 56

59 (*right*). Aragazzi Tomb. Christ Blessing.
Now set in rear wall of Duomo, Montepulciano. Michelozzo

60. Christ's hand. Detail of 59

61. Aragazzi's hands. Detail of 46

62. Aragazzi Tomb. Angel, as now positioned, to the left of high altar of the Duomo, Montepulciano. Michelozzo

63. Aragazzi Tomb. Correct front view of Angel, as originally positioned on tomb

64–65. Aragazzi Tomb. St. Michael the Archangel, front and rear view.
Now set to the right of the high altar of the Duomo, Montepulciano. Michelozzo

66. Christ Blessing. Detail of 59

67. Angel. Detail of 62

68. Head of Christ. Detail of 59

69. Head of Angel. Detail of 62

70. Portal lunette with terracotta relief
of the Virgin and Child, St. John the Baptist and St. Augustine.
Sant'Agostino, Montepulciano. Michelozzo and workshop

71 (*right*). St. Augustine. Detail of 70. Workshop of Michelozzo

72. Head of St. John the Baptist. Detail of 70. Michelozzo

73. Head of St. John the Baptist. Terracotta. Florence, Chiesa dell' Annunziata. Michelozzo

74. St. John the Baptist. Terracotta. Florence, Chiesa dell' Annunziata. Michelozzo

75. Silver Dossal of the Baptistery. Florentine, 14th and 15th centuries. Florence, Museo del' Opera del Duomo

76. St. John the Baptist
Central figure of 75. Michelozzo

77. Old photograph of 74, showing
condition of figure at beginning of this century

78. Prato, Duomo. External Pulpit. Donatello, Michelozzo and others

79–80. Prato Pulpit. Relief panels with Dancing Angels. Donatello

81–82. Prato Pulpit. Relief panels with Dancing Angels.
Workshop of Donatello and Michelozzo

83–84. Prato Pulpit. Relief panels with Dancing Angels. Donatello with workshop

85 (*below*). Prato Pulpit. Relief panel with Dancing Angels. Donatello, Michelozzo and workshop

86 (*right*). Prato Pulpit. Detail of 85

87. Prato Pulpit. Detail of 84

88. Prato Pulpit. Detail of 80

89–90.· Relief sculpture on Lavabo and detail. Florence, Museo Bardini.
Florentine, mid fifteenth century? (wrongly attributed to Michelozzo)

91. Virgin and Child. Florence, Chiesa dell' Annunziata.
Florentine, third quarter of fifteenth century (wrongly attributed to Michelozzo?)

92. The Medici Impresa. Florence, San Miniato, Cappella del Crocefisso.
Workshop of Michelozzo

Comparative Illustrations

93. Bronze Epitaph on Tomb of Bartolommeo Aragazzi. Michelozzo

94. The Marzocco. Donatello, *c.* 1418–19. Florence, Bargello

95. Effigy of Baldassare Cossa (seen from above).
Florence, Baptistery. Donatello

96. Tomb of Pope Martin V. Bronze. Florentine, c. 1431.
Rome, St. John Lateran

7. Late fifteenth-century drawing of the Cossa Tomb. *Libro* of Buonaccorso Ghiberti. Florence, Biblioteca Nazionale

98. Bronze Shrine of S. Proto, S. Giacinto and S. Nemesio. Lorenzo Ghiberti. Florence, Bargello

99. Detail from *Eugenius IV despatching Aeneas Silvius to the Emperor Frederick III.* Pinturicchio. Siena, Libreria Piccolomini

100. *Tabernacolo di Parte Guelfa.* Donatello and workshop *c.* 1424 Florence, Or San Michele

101. Tomb of Nofri Strozzi. Niccolò di Piero Lamberti, 1418–19. Florence, Santa Trinità

102. Tomb of Cardinal Francèsco Carbone.
Neapolitan, c. 1400. Naples, Duomo

103. Tomb of Cardinal Enrico Minutolo. Neapolitan,
between 1402 and 1412. Naples, Duomo, Cappella Minutolo

104. Portal of S. Giovanni dei Pappacoda,
Naples. Neapolitan, 1415

105. Tomb of King Ladislaus. Andrea di Onofrio and
assistants, 1428–32. Naples, S. Giovanni a Carbonara

106–107. Tomb of Antonio and Onofrio Penna. Framework showing frescoes, and present state. Antonio Baboccio. *c.* 1413. Naples, Santa Chiara

108. Tomb of Antonio and Onofrio Penna. Effigy and sarcophagus. Antonio Baboccio, *c.* 1413. Naples, Santa Chiara

109. Tomb of Beata Villana delle Botti. Bernardo Rossellino, 1451–52. Florence, Santa Maria Novella

110. Tomb of Doge Tommaso Mocenigo. Piero Lamberti and Giovanni di Martino da Fiesole, 1423–24. Venice, Santi Giovanni e Paolo

111. Tabernacle. Andrea Orcagna, 1349–59. Florence, Or San Michele

112. Proposed reconstruction of the Aragazzi Tomb. Ingegnere Emilio Marcucci, 1887

113. Conjectural reconstruction of the Aragazzi Tomb. Fritz Burger, 1904

114. Madonna and Child with candlestick-bearing Angels. Giovanni Pisano, c. 1305–6. Padua, Scrovegni Chapel

115. The Trinity.
Masaccio. Florence, Santa Maria Novella

116. Relief of the Virgin blessing
Queen Sancia of Naples. Tino di Camaino. Washington,
National Gallery of Art, Samuel H. Kress Collection

117. Tomb of Bishop Antonio degli Orsi. Sarcophagus
relief showing the Bishop presented by the Virgin
to Christ. Tino di Camaino, 1321. Florence, Duomo

118. Tomb of Luca Savelli (d. 1266), incorporating a Roman sarcophagus.
Rome, Santa Maria in Aracoeli

119. Detail of base from tomb of Bartolommeo Aragazzi. Workshop of
Michelozzo. Montepulciano, Duomo

120. Tomb of Cardinal Guglielmo Fieschi (d. 1256), incorporating a Roman sarcophagus of the fourth century A.D. Rome, San Lorenzo fuori le Mura

121. Roman sarcophagus showing scenes from the life of a Roman general. Mantua, Palazzo Ducale

122. Tomb of Matteo and Elisabetta Geraldini. Agostino di Duccio, 1477. Amelia, San Francesco

123. Tomb of Cardinal
Philippe d'Alençon. Roman, c. 1397.
Rome, Santa Maria in Trastevere

124. Tomb of Francesco and Niccolò dell' Anguillara.
Paolo Romano, c. 1408.
Capranica, San Francesco

125. Front of the Tomb of
Grand Admiral Luigi Aldomorisco. Antonio Baboccio,
1421. Naples, San Lorenzo Maggiore

126. The Virgin presents Aldomorisco and Ladislaus to Christ. Detail of 125

127. Canopy of the *Tabernacolo dell' Arte de' Rigattieri*, 1411. Florence, Or San Michele

128. Canopy from portal. Niccolò di Piero Lamberti, 1408–10. Florence, Or San Michele

129. Knife. Italian, fifteenth century. London, Victoria and Albert Museum

130. Sant'Antilia holding a model of Montepulciano.
Detail of Altarpiece. Taddeo di Bartolo.
Montepulciano, Duomo

131. Muleteer from 'The Virgin obtaining
the protection of Pope Calixtus III for Siena'.
Sano di Pietro. Siena, Pinacoteca Nazionale

132–133. 'Faith' and 'Hope'. Bronze figures on Font. Donatello. Siena, Duomo, Baptistery

134. Habakkuk (Lo Zuccone). Donatello, 1427–36. Florence, Campanile of the Duomo

135. St. Matthew. Ghiberti. Florence, Or San Michele

136. David. Donatello, 1408–9, 1416. Florence, Bargello

137. Virgin and Child
(Torrigiani Madonna). Florence, Bargello
(wrongly attributed to Michelozzo)

138. Virgin and Child.
Terracotta. Florence, Bargello
(wrongly attributed to Michelozzo)

139. Virgin and Child. Attributed to Michelozzo.
Florence, Bargello

140. Virgin and Child from the Tomb of Baldassare Cossa.
Michelozzo. Florence, Baptistery

1. Façade of Sant'Agostino, Montepulciano. Michelozzo, 1430–36 (top section completed 1508)

142. Prato, Duomo. External Pulpit. Donatello, Michelozzo and others, 1428–38

List of Illustrations

F

431

Index

Figures in italics refer to illustrations.
The Index does not include references to Documents, beginning on page 289,
nor to Chronologies of Donatello and Michelozzo, beginning on page 321.

435